100 Best
Log Home
Floor Plans

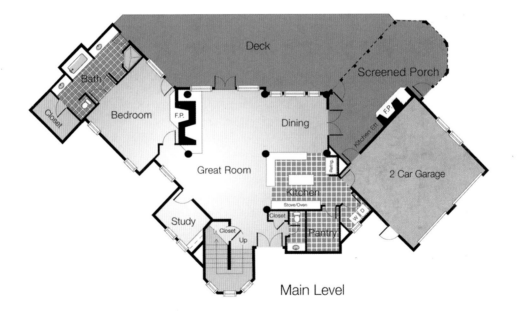

Main Level

from the editor of

LOG HOMES ILLUSTRATED

Roland Sweet

©2007 Krause Publications

Published by

An Imprint of F+W Publications

700 East State Street • Iola, WI 54990-0001
715-445-2214 • 888-457-2873
www.krausebooks.com

Our toll-free number to place an order or obtain a free catalog is (800) 258-0929.

ON THE COVER:
Showcased on the front cover is The Kuhns Bros. Log Homes "Chesapeake" model, featuring three front dormers, two rear dormers, porches and decks. Find out more inside. (The color rendering of the home is courtesy of Kuhns Bros. Log Homes)

Library of Congress Control Number: 2007923821
ISBN 13: 978-089689-496-9
ISBN 10: 0-89689-496-7

Designed by Donna Mummery
Edited by Joe Kertzman

Printed in China

Contents

INTRODUCTION

Bringing Your Ideas

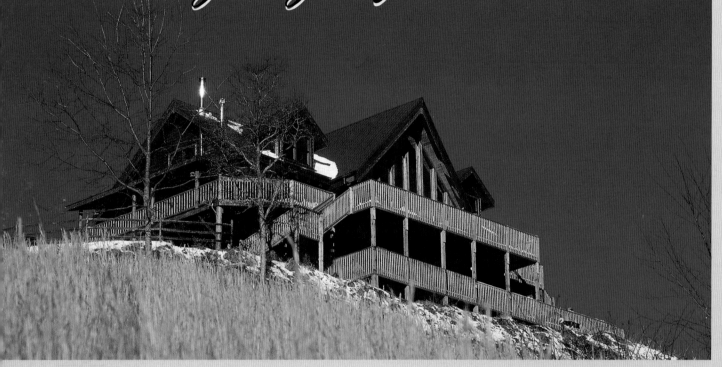

Log homes continue their unprecedented appeal. They remain popular as second homes and primary residences. Logs represent the one category in building materials that people can become excited about, romanticize about, rhapsodize and fantasize. Log homes aren't just places to live, but they represent a way of life, one to which many Americans aspire.

A big advantage of owning a log home is the opportunity to take part in planning the home. The process isn't all that different from designing one of numerous other kinds of homes. It begins with translating your ideas to paper or onto a computer screen. A house plan consists of two elements: the layout, or floor plan, showing the size and relationship of the rooms, and the elevations that depict how the home will look three-dimensionally. Similar layouts can showcase several elevations.

How you allocate the space in your home depends on your budget, your building site, your family size and how you intend to live in your home. Start with the basic premise: how many rooms do you want and how big will they be?

Once you've decided that, turn your attention to the features of the structure that will define it as a log home. How you distribute the wood, balancing it with your taste in glass, stone, maybe some drywall or vertical paneling and floors, will distinguish the interior of your log home from others.

Most log homes feature certain design elements that define them as log homes. These aren't necessarily unique to log homes, but they are more common in

to Life

them than in other styles of homes. Among these are open layouts with great rooms that combine living, dining and kitchen space; big country kitchens; lofts and cathedral ceilings; walls of windows that allow natural light in and face the best views; wide decks; casual porches; master bedroom suites; and proud staircases.

These hallmarks of contemporary log-home design replace the antiquated notion that the interiors of log homes are dark, cramped and dreary. More airy elements are often difficult to visualize when applying them to log-home design. The best way to grasp them is to become familiar with modern plans and layouts.

You're always working within a footprint, big or small, so look for ideas that can be achieved in the allotted space. Simple floor plans showing where the walls go provide clues about how homes look and "live" inside, with few hallways and other closed-off areas.

To get a sense of laying out a log home, consider the origin and evolution of log-home design. Begin with a square or rectangle. That's your basic pioneer log cabin. The walls were as long as the trees people could chop down and as tall as the number of trees they were able to fell and stack. They hoisted the timber into place by hand, fashioning the walls of their solid-wood, on-the-spot homes. A hardy pioneer might have managed a 12-by-12-foot cabin, while two or three men working together aspired to 20-by-20-foot houses.

The first modification to the basic one-room floor plan was in the division of living space from sleeping space. Barn-like lofts appeared, and at this stage, even in civilized settlements, kitchens and bathrooms remained separate entities from the house.

Two Pens Equal One Dogtrot

One early variation of log-home design was the dogtrot. A basic one-room cabin was called a pen. The dogtrot combined two pens, side by side, with a connecting breezeway. As it evolved, the breezeway was usually enclosed to become part of the interior space. Eventually, two-story log houses appeared.

People began buying log homes—no longer cabins—and moving into them as primary residences. Even people seeking simplicity expected more bathrooms and closets, and airy, large-looking kitchens. Engineering was able to satisfy people's demands for a variety of layout possibilities.

The demand for unconventional space within designs prompted log home manufacturers to develop an assortment of plans that would attract potential new customers.

Which design works for you will depend a lot on your building site, not just your property in general, but exactly where on that property you intend to build your home—the most advantageous vantage point.

Wise buyers wait to purchase land before shopping for plans. A higher percentage of log homes over regular homes are built on sloping sites. Log homes, more than any other style, extend beyond the walls and greet the outdoors. Don't pick a plan only to discover that, by integrating it, you turn your back on the land's best features.

It helps to remember that not all the walls inside a log home have to be log. Framed walls are cheaper and more versatile than log walls, and log walls can get complicated without thorough planning. A common arrangement is the interior cruciform, which essentially divides the log box twice, enclosing some rooms in all-log walls, but others with subdivided space and framed walls, build-outs and closets.

Familiarize yourself with as many floor plans as you can. *100 Best Log Home Floor Plans* provides a foundation of knowledge that can lead to your final version of the ideal log home.

Versatile, Livable Plans

The leading log-home manufacturers submitted their best plans, defined as those that are the most popular for customers seeking practical or innovative solutions to their allocations of space. They aren't fanciful notions but actual plans offered by companies that have resulted in homes being built and lived in, not just once but repeatedly. Most of the plans are versatile enough to be modified and meet customers' wants and needs.

As you review the plans in *100 Best Log Home Floor Plans*, keep certain principles in mind. They can save you time in trial and error.

The great-room concept is a frequent starting point for log-home plans. Many decisions go into laying out this central open space, which combines living, dining and kitchen areas. Open spaces often rely on accent posts and beams to provide visual separation.

When you're looking at floor plans, notice how different spaces relate to each other. Log homes do have interior walls, framed or log, according to your taste and budget, but typically lack hallways. Also, if you have a worthy view, you'll find yourself leaning toward big windows, perhaps an entire wall of them, to provide a strong focal point.

Views are why buying your land before you shop for a plan makes sense. Fortunately, engineering advances permit window placement pretty much anywhere in a log wall. Being able to control the flow of natural light throughout the home is a welcome opportunity for people who previously considered the interiors of log homes too dark.

Lofts remain a popular feature of log homes, especially in layouts without a lot of bedrooms. Lofts make great guest quarters, home offices and hobby rooms that can be closed off or left open. Another purpose of lofts is to allow overhead space in the living room for cathedral ceilings.

Big Kitchens Are A Country Tradition

Today, big kitchens are a country tradition that many people associate with log homes. If you anticipate your family or company joining you from the other rooms, find a plan that promotes flow and accommodates a crowd.

Separate dining rooms are a strong preference among people who want a more formal eating space. Otherwise, including an open dining area adjacent to the kitchen and living room promotes an air of informality that people find appealing about log homes.

Entryways are another focal point. Foyers cut into usable space, so add pizzazz or function. Some people like front doors that open right into the living room. Others prefer a more gradual transition. A common motif is having an entry that uses a different flooring material, something suited for coming in from outdoors, especially in nasty weather, or steps down into the living area.

Anterooms or entry hallways can accommodate stairs, preventing the intrusion of stairs into living rooms and allowing them to have their own design and décor. Remember, anytime you build up or down, some of your square footage will go toward stairs, as much as a wall's worth of space.

Cathedral ceilings are not limited to great rooms in log homes. They are common over second-floor master bedrooms, or, if the roof is tall and steep enough, a loft ceiling can be incorporated, in almost split-level fashion, in the great room.

Shorter second-floor ceilings cry out for dormers. They add expense but reduce accidental head banging and allow the sunlight to shine in while breaking up the roof's mass, all without adding to the home's footprint. Dormers can be sided with logs.

Think about bedrooms. In years gone by, people tended to group all sleeping quarters together. Nowadays, people favor separating the master bedroom, which often expands to become a master suite or even a master wing. Because so many log-home buyers are middle-aged or older, many prefer their bedroom be on the main level. Guest rooms work well on upper or lower levels, or even above attached or detached garages. If you're planning on plenty of grandchildren visiting, consider the bunkroom concept.

Bathrooms are a necessity, but they can be an extravagance, not just in their individual size and appointments, but also in their number. Regardless of size or number, locate them strategically.

Allow ample space for water heaters and other mechanical systems. Where will the washer-dryer go? And keep track of how much storage space you'll want, especially for recreational gear, such as snow skis, which not only have to be kept ready during the season, but also removed from sight at other times.

The size and placement of these common log-home features are your choice, based on the size of the home you want and the way you anticipate living in it. There is very little you can envision that a log home cannot be designed to provide. That's why it's important to familiarize yourself with a variety of designs to determine which one suits you best or is a good starting point for your custom design.

The plans in this book address most people's needs. They represent traditional log-home layout, current home-plan trends and future possibilities. We've arranged them by size rather than style but caution you that any layout can be enlarged or reduced to meet your needs. For more information about specific plans, please contact the log-home company listed.

—Roland Sweet

Small Talk About Cozy

Featured log homes include those sized under 2,000 square feet

Homes under 2,000 square feet can be every bit the equal of larger ones. Living in a smaller log home doesn't mean sacrificing any of the comfort that you expect from a log dwelling. In fact, the small home offers an opportunity to create the special charm that recalls yesteryear's log cabins while enjoying all the design features, amenities and energy efficiency associated with today's full-size homes.

The key to successfully designing a small home begins by recognizing the square-footage limits of your budget and working within them. Conflicts usually arise because most people who want a small home expect too many of the features found in larger dwellings. You just have to take the time to fit it all in.

Buyers of small homes still want a large living area and large kitchen, master bedroom suites with large baths and walk-in closets. The one thing that most of them don't think of and plan for is storage space.

In designing a small home, consider your basic needs first. Determine where you will be spending most of your

Log Homes

time. If you spend a lot of time in your bedroom reading, watching television or perhaps have a computer desk there, you'll need to make the bedroom a practical size. If you spend more time in the living area or kitchen, your bedrooms can be smaller.

When deciding how many bedrooms, bathrooms, closets and such that you'll need and their sizes, don't overlook the benefits of a basement. Putting utilities, a washer and dryer, even a spare bedroom or work room in a finished basement will free up space on the main level, giving you more room to work with—and for a lot less money than a second story would cost.

An open floor plan will also maximize your available space. Having the living, dining and kitchen areas with no dividing walls works well in a small room. Also, having a vaulted or cathedral ceiling area gives more open feel to smaller spaces.

If possible, design the plan to have short hallways. Long hallways are wasted space. Give much consideration to the location and space for stairs to the loft or basement since they will consume about 35 to 40 square feet of floor space.

Despite needing to bring your wishes into line with your budget, buying a small home doesn't necessarily mean making sacrifices. More likely, the issue is balancing the two. And there is a big plus for small homes. The small home will generally be less complicated. Roof design, bearing points and spans of structural framing members are all areas where buyers can conserve to gain the best value for their money.

Finally, don't pass up ideas gleaned from studying large log homes. Every picture holds details that may add charm to any size home. And, believe it or not, successful large homes get the most efficient use of the space. If nothing else, you might find some good decorating ideas, particularly for coordinating colors with logs.

By giving careful consideration to making the best use of the space available, you will arrive at a plan that not only meets your budget but also exceeds your expectations. And that is the goal of every log home.

Buyers can get the most for their money by following these guidelines:

- Keep small rooms bright, using windows, lighting and wall and ceiling coverings

- Plan rooms for multiple uses

- Use every nook and cranny available for storage space, such as under staircases and the eaves in loft areas

- If space is tight, delete the cathedral ceiling over the great room. Despite the wonderful look, it wastes square footage. An extra bedroom or a spacious master suite could be located above a living room with a standard-height ceiling

The Roberts

Despite its modest size—at 1,471 square feet—The Roberts would make an ideal year-round home for a young family or retired couple.

Plan Title: The Roberts

Home Size: 1,471 square feet

Plan Designer: Northeastern Log Homes

For more, contact
Northeastern Log Homes, Kenduskeag, Maine;
phone: 800-624-2797;
website: www.northeasternlog.com.

The home's modest size suggests its suitability as a second home, but it is also ideal for a retired couple or young family as a permanent, year-round residence. Either way, the plan manages to accommodate a master suite with a roomy walk-in closet and its own deck, and two other bedrooms.

Its most striking feature is the prow configuration of the living room, which allows for ample glass to let in light. Behind a central fireplace, the dining area and kitchen are tucked away side by side.

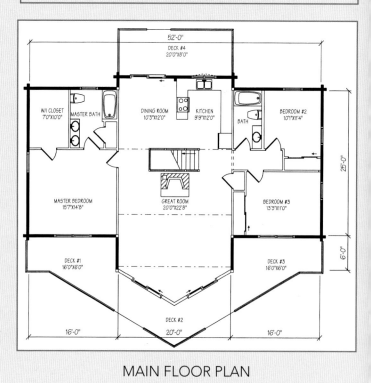

MAIN FLOOR PLAN

Pictured is the dining room of The Roberts, part of an open concept, or great room. Note the exposed beams.

The prow configuration of the living room is the most striking feature of The Roberts.

The fireplace is the main focal point of The Roberts living room.

The plan accommodates a master suite with its own deck.

The Tucker

The inset porch and dormer are distinguishable features of the compact Tucker log home model.

Plan Title: **Tucker**

Home Size: **1,880 square feet**

Plan Designer: **Appalachian Log Structures**

For more information, contact Appalachian Log Structures, Ripley, West Virginia; phone: 800-458-9990; website: www.applog.com.

Exterior features visually enlarge this otherwise compact home. Such features include the inset porch, a peaked roof over the living room and a dormer that mimics its pitch. Inside, the plan accommodates a first-floor and two upper-level bedrooms.

The living room fills both levels and is topped off with a beamed cathedral ceiling that conveys airiness. The kitchen adjoins a utility room and opens into the dining or family room with a comforting fireplace. A rear dormer tops a porch that stretches the width of the house, with access to the porch off the dining room.

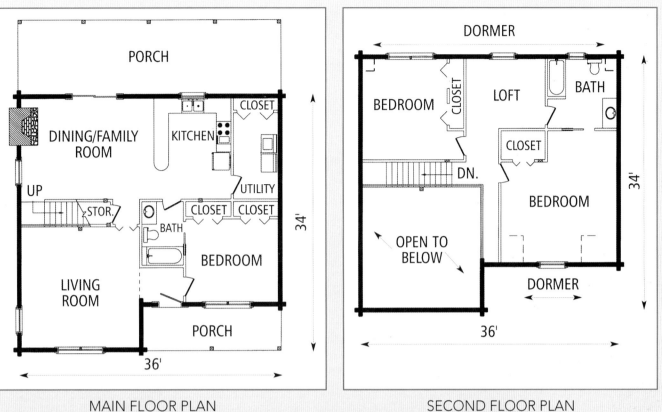

PORCH

DINING/FAMILY ROOM

KITCHEN

CLOSET

UP

STOR.

BATH

UTILITY

CLOSET   CLOSET

LIVING ROOM

BEDROOM

PORCH

36'

34'

MAIN FLOOR PLAN

DORMER

BEDROOM

CLOSET

LOFT

BATH

CLOSET

DN.

OPEN TO BELOW

BEDROOM

DORMER

36'

34'

SECOND FLOOR PLAN

A dormer mimics the pitch of the peaked roof over the living room.

Plans Under 2,000 Square Feet · **13**

The Greenbrier II

Multiple rooflines, overhangs and extensions give the Greenbrier II the appearance of being larger than its 1,752 square feet.

Plan Title: **Greenbrier II**

Home Size: **1,752 square feet**

Plan Designer: **Appalachian Log Structures**

For more information, contact
Appalachian Log Structures, Ripley, West Virginia;
phone: 800-458-9990;
website: www.applog.com.

Small in scale, yet designed with an airy feeling, this plan creates an atmosphere of space and fills the home with light. Two bedrooms and a full bath upstairs lead to a balcony overlooking the spacious great room below.

Downstairs, the great room spills out onto a 28-foot deck. A well-planned flow keeps the living area feeling anything but compact. Even though the master bedroom and living room are open above, the loft still accommodates two bedrooms and a bath.

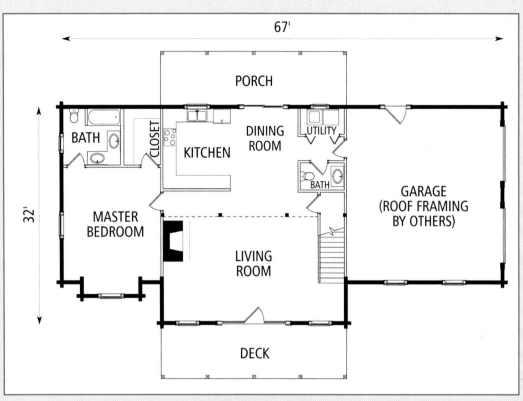

MAIN FLOOR PLAN

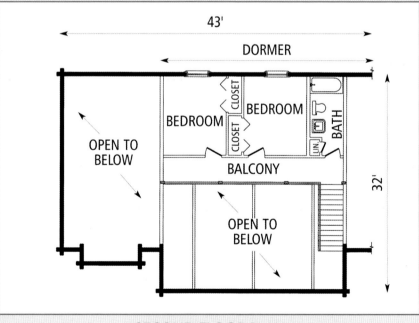

SECOND FLOOR PLAN

The Fairfield

The two gable dormers in front and shed dormer in the rear of The Fairfield help expand headroom and make the most of its small footprint.

Plan Title: **The Fairfield**

Home Size: **1,278 square feet**

Plan Designer: **Coventry Log Homes**

For more information, contact
Coventry Log Homes, Woodsville, New Hampshire;
phone: 800-308-7505;
website: www.coventryloghomes.com.

This plan makes the most of its small footprint by adding a loft with two bedrooms and a bath, relying on two gable dormers in front and a 32-foot-long shed dormer in the rear to expand usable headroom. Leaving the space above the living area open enhances the plan's openness. The first-floor bathroom, which serves the master bedroom, is anything but compact, providing nearly 100 square feet.

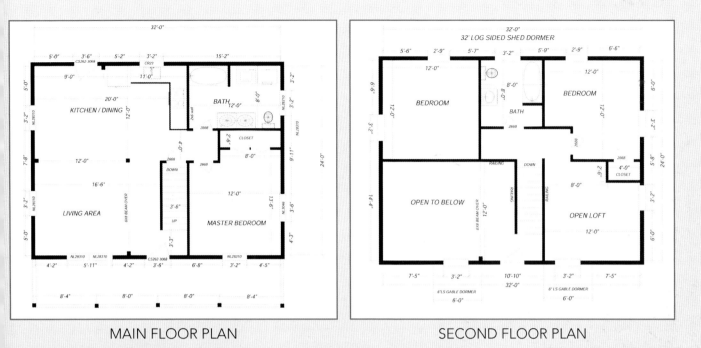

MAIN FLOOR PLAN

SECOND FLOOR PLAN

The open concept of the living room is a nice touch and gives the interior of the home a larger-than-it-really-is look and feel.

No partitions between the dining room/kitchen and living room add to the open feel of The Fairfield.

Cabin Fever

At 1,178 square feet, the Alpine Log Homes "Cabin Fever" is modest in size, yet it features a large back deck that wraps around one side of the house and connects with the front porch.

Plan Title: Cabin Fever

Home Size: 1,178 square feet

Plan Designer: Alpine Log Homes

For more information, contact
Alpine Log Homes, Victor, Montana;
phone: 406-642-3451;
website: www.alpineloghomes.com.

The basis of this modest, two-story plan is a "T" shape. Two bedrooms and two baths with a loft above form the crossbar of the "T," while the great room occupies the stem. Central to the layout is a kitchen that faces out to the living area.

Vaulted ceilings add volume to both bedrooms, which also showcase window seats. A special feature of the master bath is access to an outdoor shower on the side deck. A larger deck wraps around the back and other side and connects to the front porch. The two porches capture a wide panoramic view.

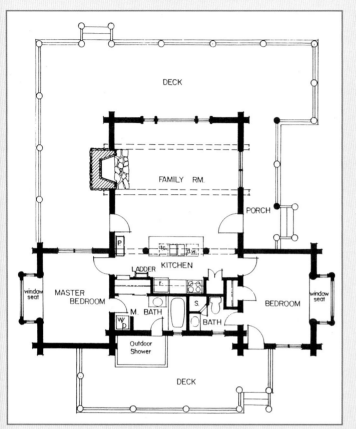

MAIN FLOOR PLAN

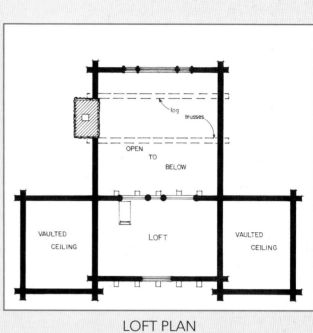

LOFT PLAN

Central to the layout of the Cabin Fever model is a kitchen that faces out to the living area.

The basis of this modest, two-story plan is a "T" shape. Two bedrooms and two baths with a loft above form the crossbar of the "T," while the great room (shown) occupies the stem.

Rockbridge

Elaborate windows add to the contemporary feel of the Southland Log Homes "Rockbridge" model.

Plan Title: Rockbridge

Home Size: 1,724 square feet

Plan Designer: Southland Log Homes

For more information, contact
Southland Log Homes, Irmo, South Carolina;
phone: 800-828-1492;
website: www.southlandloghomes.com.

Elaborate windows add a contemporary feel to this layout, which features two master bedroom suites, one occupying the loft and the other on the main level. The bulk of the loft level is dedicated to storage, but it includes a sitting area overlooking the great room. The lower level has a third bedroom and a U-shaped kitchen open to the living and dining areas. A covered entry transitions to a 516-square-foot side deck and rear porch.

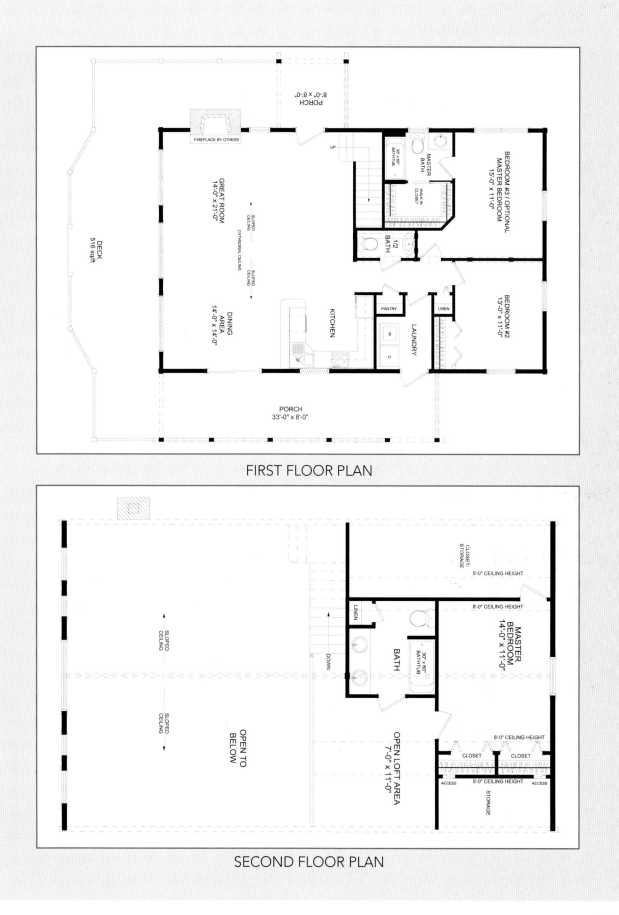

FIRST FLOOR PLAN

SECOND FLOOR PLAN

Madison

The Southland Log Homes Madison model comes complete with a garage, laundry room, kitchen, dining room and great room, and for anyone who likes to entertain, the home also features front and rear porches and a deck.

Plan Title: **Madison**

Home Size: **1,804 square feet**

Plan Designer: **Southland Log Homes**

For more information, contact Southland Log Homes, Irmo, South Carolina; phone: 800-828-1492; website: www.southlandloghomes.com.

One-story living makes this plan attractive for a getaway or retirement home. The living and dining areas of the great room enjoy cathedral ceilings and front and rear porches. Next to this space is a small hall connecting two bedrooms and a bath.

Opposite are the kitchen and the master bedroom, with the master bedroom heading through facing walk-in closets to a roomy bath next to the garage. The garage enters the house through a hallway that connects to a coat closet and laundry room, the latter of which opens to the rear deck.

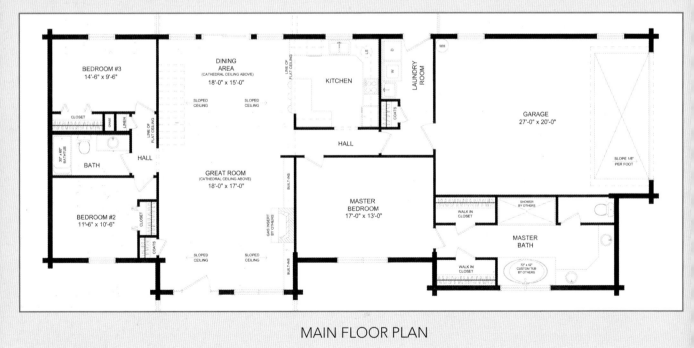

MAIN FLOOR PLAN

The Carriage House

A color rendering of "The Carriage House" gives a good, visual idea of how the loft apartment rests above the garage and workshop.

Plan Title: The Carriage House

Home Size: 1,008 square feet

Plan Designer: Log Homes of America

For more information, contact
Log Homes of America,
Banner Elk, North Carolina;
phone: 828-963-7777;
website: www.loghomesofamerica.com.

This studio apartment is ideal for a getaway or guesthouse. A shed dormer adds headroom to the living and kitchen area, and its triplet windows let in ample light. The compact-but-efficient layout features the essentials, plus a washer-dryer closet and low storage. Access is through a shop that is partitioned from the two-bay garage.

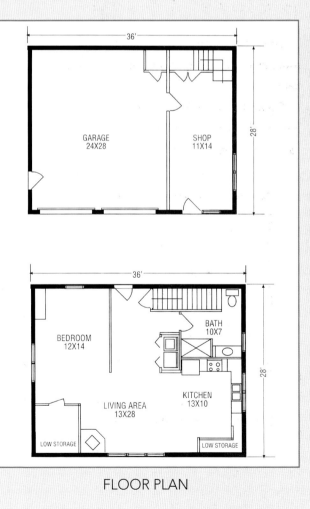

GARAGE
24X28

SHOP
11X14

36'

28'

BEDROOM
12X14

BATH
10X7

KITCHEN
13X10

LIVING AREA
13X28

LOW STORAGE

LOW STORAGE

36'

28'

FLOOR PLAN

Juliana

To the left of the front porch of the Gastineau Log Homes "Juliana" model, the roomy master suite occupies more than a third of the main level. To the right of the porch is the great room.

Plan Title: **Juliana**

Home Size: **1,881 square feet**

Plan Designer: **Gastineau Log Homes**

For more information, contact Gastineau Log Homes, New Bloomfield, Missouri; phone: 800-654-9253; website: www.oakloghome.com.

The roomy master suite of the Gastineau Log Homes Juliana occupies more than a third of the main level and includes a sitting area that could serve as a home office. A generous laundry room is located off the dining area, opposite the efficiently arranged corner kitchen.

A central stairway defines the boundary of the great room, whose front-facing windows fill the home with light. Upstairs, dormers brighten the second and third bedrooms.

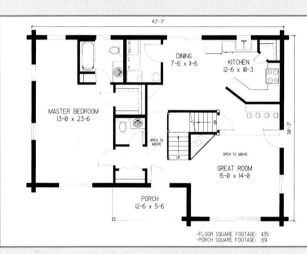

MAIN FLOOR PLAN

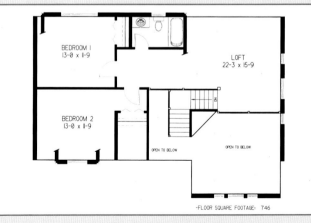

SECOND FLOOR PLAN

Ideal when situated on land with a nice front view, the Caroline's open prow design with trapezoidal windows takes full advantage of the scenery.

Plan Title: **Caroline**

Home Size: **1,807 square feet**

Plan Designer: **Gastineau Log Homes**

For more information, contact
Gastineau Log Homes, New Bloomfield, Missouri;
phone: 800-654-9253;
website: www.oakloghome.com.

The open prow design with exposed beam trusses and grand, trapezoidal windows takes full advantage of a view. The interior design also incorporates a long great room that leads to the kitchen, which, in turn, accesses a rear porch.

The large main-floor master suite features a beamed ceiling, large walk-in closet and a luxurious bathroom. The utility room is conveniently located across the hall, through the powder room. Dormers on the second floor allow for two large bedrooms and a full bath. One of the bedrooms enjoys a private balcony.

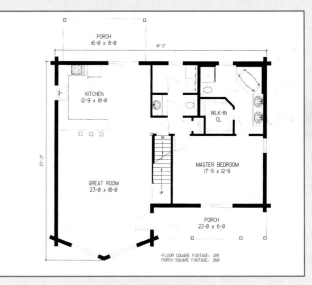

FIRST FLOOR PLAN

SECOND FLOOR PLAN

Chaparral

The front porch of the Gastineau Log Homes "Chaparral" model is situated between the garage (right) and two bedrooms to the left.

Plan Title: **Chaparral**

Home Size: **1,916 square feet**

Plan Designer: **Gastineau Log Homes**

For more information, contact
Gastineau Log Homes, New Bloomfield, Missouri;
phone: 800-654-9253; website: www.oakloghome.com.

The front door leads from the covered porch into a living room that merges with a family room and dining area. An angled hall leads to the bedroom area. A highlight is the master suite, entered through double doors to reveal a cathedral ceiling and integrated master bath with a whirlpool tub surrounded by windows. This roomy haven accesses the wide deck, which is ideal for entertaining. Abundant windows flood the home's interior with light.

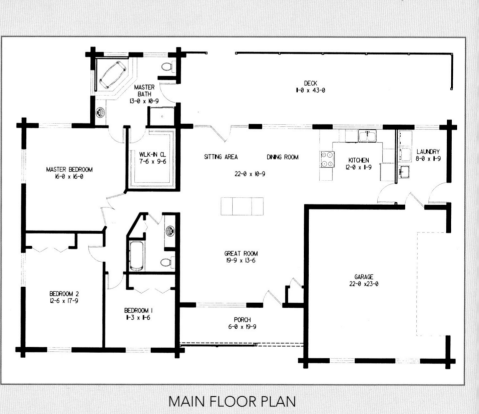

MAIN FLOOR PLAN

The front door of the Gastineau Log Homes Chaparral leads from the covered porch into a living room that merges with a family room and dining area.

Several skylights and windows allow plenty of light into the kitchen.

A highlight of the Chaparral is the master suite, entered through double doors to reveal a cathedral ceiling and integrated master bath with a whirlpool tub surrounded by windows.

Wintergreen CV#1

Walls of windows flank a large stone chimney.

Plan Title: Wintergreen CV#1

Home Size: 1,831 square feet

Plan Designer: Golden Eagle Log Homes

For more information, contact
Golden Eagle Log Homes,
Wisconsin Rapids, Wisconsin;
phone: 800-270-5025;
website: www.goldeneagleloghomes.com.

This cozy three-bedroom plan offers a few space surprises, notably a sunroom projecting off the dining area to provide open views in all directions. There's also a sizable laundry room in the hallway leading to the garage.

A dormer in the great room brings in extra light to enlarge the sense of openness. The unconventionally arranged loft and kitchen below maximize the space, aided by a bump out, which allows extra windows to brighten the kitchen sink area.

The unconventionally arranged loft and kitchen below maximize the space, aided by a bump out, which allows extra windows to brighten the kitchen sink area.

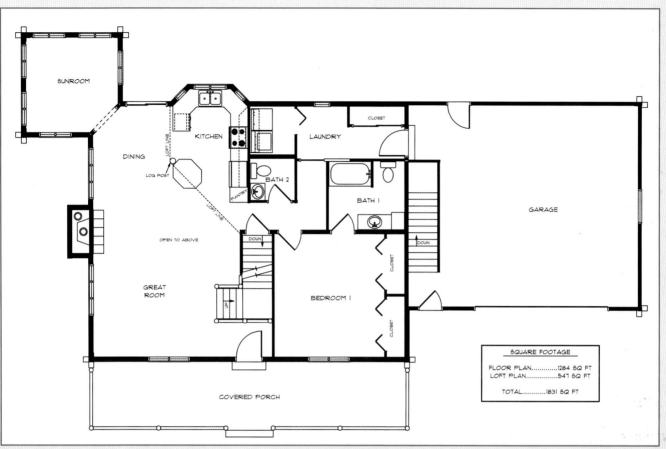

FIRST FLOOR PLAN

SUNROOM

DINING

KITCHEN

LOFT LINE

LOG POST

LOFT LINE

PANTRY

BATH 2

LAUNDRY

CLOSET

BATH 1

GARAGE

OPEN TO ABOVE

DOWN

GREAT ROOM

UP

BEDROOM 1

CLOSET

DOWN

CLOSET

COVERED PORCH

SQUARE FOOTAGE

FLOOR PLAN.............1284 SQ FT
LOFT PLAN..............547 SQ FT

TOTAL............1831 SQ FT

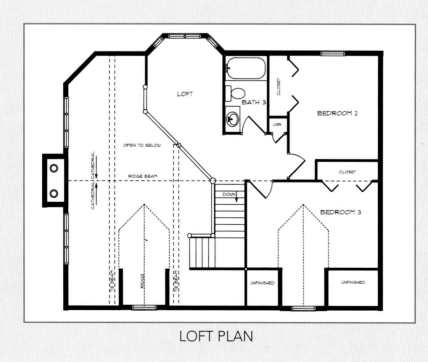

LOFT PLAN

LOFT

BATH 3

CLOSET

BEDROOM 2

OPEN TO BELOW

CATHEDRAL/CATHEDRAL

RIDGE BEAM

LINEN

CLOSET

DOWN

TIE BEAM

RIDGE

TIE BEAM

UNFINISHED

UNFINISHED

BEDROOM 3

Beck

The practical Kuhns Bros. Log Homes "Beck" model features one level for living and a second for sleeping.

Plan Title: **Beck**

Home Size: **1,909 square feet**

Plan Designer: **Kuhns Bros. Log Homes**

For more information, contact
Kuhns Bros. Log Homes, Lewisburg, Pennsylvania;
phone: 800-326-9614;
website: www.kuhnsbros.com.

This practical plan features one level for living and a second for sleeping. Besides the open kitchen, dining area and living room, the main level offers a formal entry, bonus study and mudroom.

On the second level, side-by-side gable dormers enlarge the headroom in the loft and second bedroom. A single gable dormer brings room and light to the master bedroom, which leads to a roomy walk-in closet and turns the corner to a spacious bathroom. A smaller bedroom shares the same bathroom.

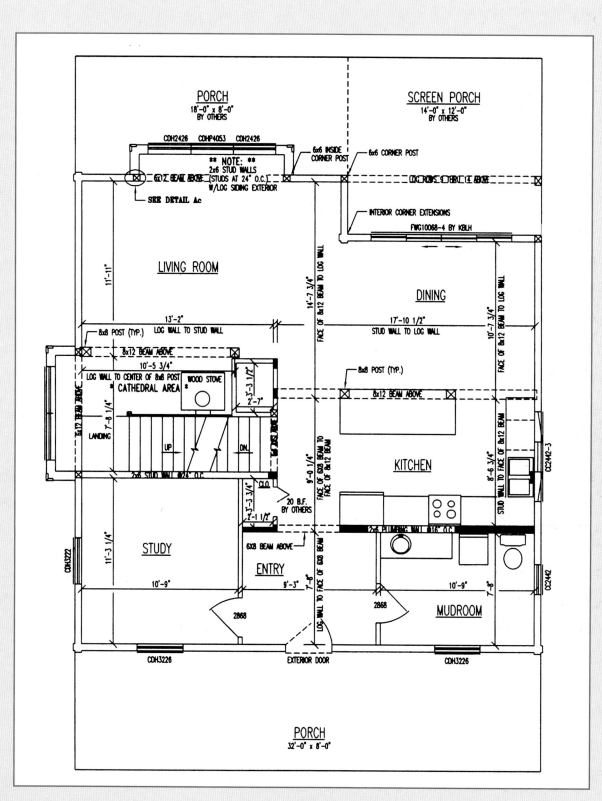

FIRST FLOOR PLAN

Beck

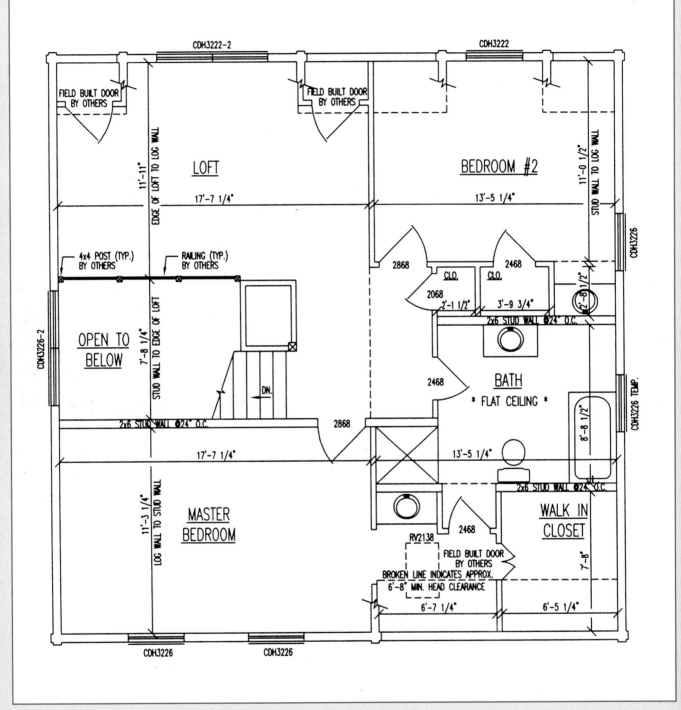

CDH3222-2   CDH3222

FIELD BUILT DOOR
BY OTHERS

FIELD BUILT DOOR
BY OTHERS

LOFT

11'-11"   EDGE OF LOFT TO LOG WALL

17'-7 1/4"

BEDROOM #2

13'-5 1/4"

11'-0 1/2"   STUD WALL TO LOG WALL

CDH3226

4x4 POST (TYP.)
BY OTHERS

RAILING (TYP.)
BY OTHERS

OPEN TO
BELOW

7'-8 1/4"   STUD WALL TO EDGE OF LOFT

CDH3226-2

2868

CLO.

CLO.

2468

2068

2'-1 1/2"

3'-9 3/4"

2'-8 1/2"

2x6 STUD WALL @24" O.C.

DN.

2868

2468

2x6 STUD WALL @24" O.C.

17'-7 1/4"

MASTER
BEDROOM

11'-3 1/4"   LOG WALL TO STUD WALL

BATH
* FLAT CEILING *

13'-5 1/4"

CDH3226 TEMP.

8'-8 1/2"

2x6 STUD WALL @24" O.C.

WALK IN
CLOSET

7'-8"

RV2138

FIELD BUILT DOOR
BY OTHERS
BROKEN LINE INDICATES APPROX.
6'-8" MIN. HEAD CLEARANCE

2468

6'-7 1/4"

6'-5 1/4"

CDH3226   CDH3226

SECOND FLOOR PLAN

Though part of an open-concept scheme, the living room has a homey feel and remains its own entity.

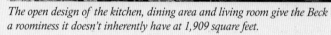

The open design of the kitchen, dining area and living room give the Beck a roominess it doesn't inherently have at 1,909 square feet.

More than one bedroom shares the spacious upstairs bathroom of the Beck.

Peacock

A color rendering of the Log Homes of America "Peacock" plan shows how the extension of the great room provides a convenient front entry and allows for full-length doors that open to the deck and let in light.

Plan Title: Peacock

Home Size: 1,768 square feet

Plan Designer: Log Homes of America

For more information, contact Log Homes of America, Banner Elk, North Carolina; phone: 828-963-7777; website: www.loghomesofamerica.com.

Bumping out the basic log-home rectangle in this one-story plan to extend the great room provides a convenient front entry. It also allows for full-length doors that open to the deck and let in light to visually enlarge the open interior space. Despite the small footprint, the plan accommodates a roomy master suite, which accesses its own porch, and even sets aside space for an enclosed laundry room in the cozy guest-room wing.

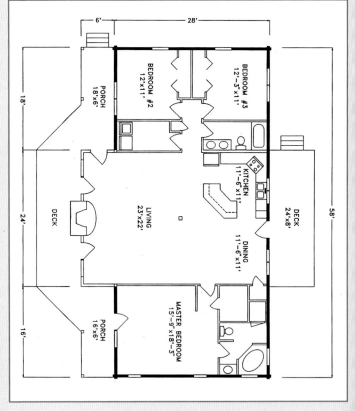

MAIN FLOOR PLAN

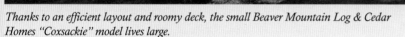

Thanks to an efficient layout and roomy deck, the small Beaver Mountain Log & Cedar Homes "Coxsackie" model lives large.

Plan Title: **The Coxsackie**

Home Size: **1,388 square feet**

Plan Designer: **Beaver Mountain Log & Cedar Homes**

For more information, contact
Beaver Mountain Log & Cedar Homes, Hancock, New York;
phone: 800-233-2770;
website: www.beavermtn.com.

This small plan lives large, thanks to its efficient layout and roomy deck. Noteworthy, too, is the generous master suite. The open living room and dining area share a cathedral ceiling and wall of windows flanking a towering fireplace. A back porch leads off the mudroom, which is next to a second full bath. An open but roomy loft overlooking the great room offers versatility.

MAIN FLOOR PLAN

LOFT PLAN

Hawks Nest

Though the main level of the Log Homes of America "Hawks Nest" devotes nearly half the square footage to a bedroom with a large walk-in closet, stairs behind the fireplace intrude as little as possible, leaving the great room open.

Plan Title: **Hawks Nest**

Home Size: **1,764 square feet**

Plan Designer: **Log Homes of America**

For more information, contact
Log Homes of America,
Banner Elk, North Carolina;
phone: 828-963-7777;
website: www.loghomesofamerica.com.

A roomy loft is ideal for the master suite or to pamper guests. The main level devotes nearly half the square footage to a bedroom with a large walk-in closet. Stairs are tucked behind the fireplace to intrude as little as possible, leaving the great room open, with the kitchen and dining areas sheltered beneath the loft. The downstairs bathroom is positioned to allow for an enclosed washer-dryer behind the tub.

The extended roofline of the "Hawks Nest" covers a good portion of the full, wraparound deck.

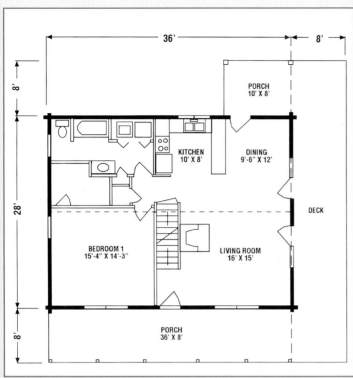

MAIN FLOOR PLAN

Dimensions on Main Floor Plan:
36'
8'
8'
28'
8'

PORCH
10' X 8'

KITCHEN
10' X 8'

DINING
9'-6" X 12'

DECK

BEDROOM 1
15'-4" X 14'-3"

LIVING ROOM
16' X 15'

PORCH
36' X 8'

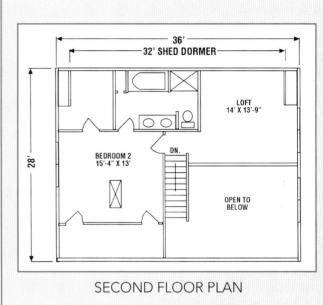

SECOND FLOOR PLAN

36'
32' SHED DORMER
28'

LOFT
14' X 13'-9"

BEDROOM 2
15'-4" X 13'

DN.

OPEN TO
BELOW

The kitchen and dining areas of the Log Homes of America "Hawks Nest" are sheltered beneath the loft.

A roomy loft is ideal for the master suite or as a room for pampering guests.

The Wyoming

The canopy-like roof of "The Wyoming" from Yellowstone Log Homes covers the wraparound deck and extends the living space beyond the log walls.

Plan Title: The Wyoming

Home Size: 1,750 square feet

Plan Designer: Yellowstone Log Homes

For more, contact
Yellowstone Log Homes, Rigby, Idaho;
phone: 208-745-8108;
website: www.yellowstoneloghomes.com.

A canopy-like roof covering the wraparound deck extends the home's living space beyond the log walls. The compact great room occupies half of the main level, allowing the other half to accommodate a roomy master suite, including a bathroom with corner tub and separate shower, and a generous laundry/mud room. The upper level holds two bedrooms, a bath and a loft area overlooking the great room.

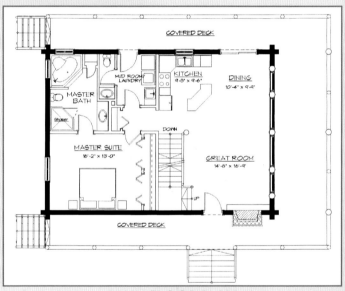

MAIN FLOOR PLAN

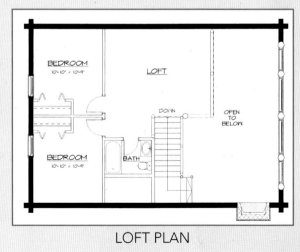

LOFT PLAN

The charming twin dormers of "The Bridger" from Yellowstone Log Homes, and a side bay window serving the dining room, bulk up the compact layout and use space efficiently.

Plan Title: **The Bridger**

Home Size: **1,060 square feet**

Plan Designer: **Yellowstone Log Homes**

For more, contact
Yellowstone Log Homes, Rigby, Idaho; phone:
208-745-8108;
website: www.yellowstoneloghomes.com.

Charming twin dormers and a side bay window serving the dining room bulk up a compact layout that uses space efficiently. The main level, for example, has an open great room sharing space with a bedroom and bath. The U-shaped kitchen shares the openness.

A deck and a country porch offer additional living space and enhance the home's good looks. Upstairs, the generous loft overlooks the great room and adjoins a modest but private master suite.

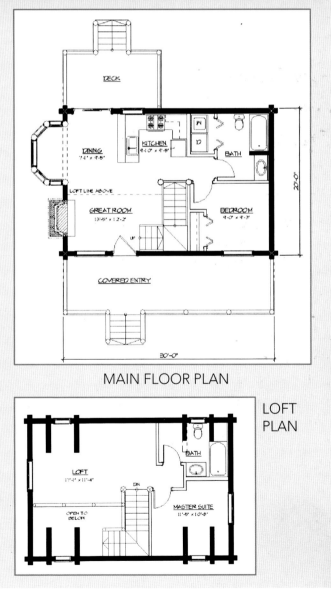

MAIN FLOOR PLAN

LOFT PLAN

The Ledgewood

Porches and dormers add to the prominence of the 1,728-square-foot Ledgewood.

Plan Title: **The Ledgewood**

Home Size: **1,728 square feet**

Plan Designer: **Coventry Log Homes**

For more information, contact Coventry Log Homes, Woodsville, New Hampshire; phone: 800-308-7505; website: www.coventryloghomes.com.

This compact plan illustrates the power of porches and dormers to add prominence. Three gable dormers in front and a shed dormer out back vary the roofline, and the wrap-around porch extends the roof well over the walls. The loft is small but fits in two ample bedrooms with big closets.

A small nook next to the bathroom overlooks the living area and entrance below. The master bedroom is on the main level, partitioned from the living area, half of which benefits from the upper-level windows of the 12-foot-wide center dormer.

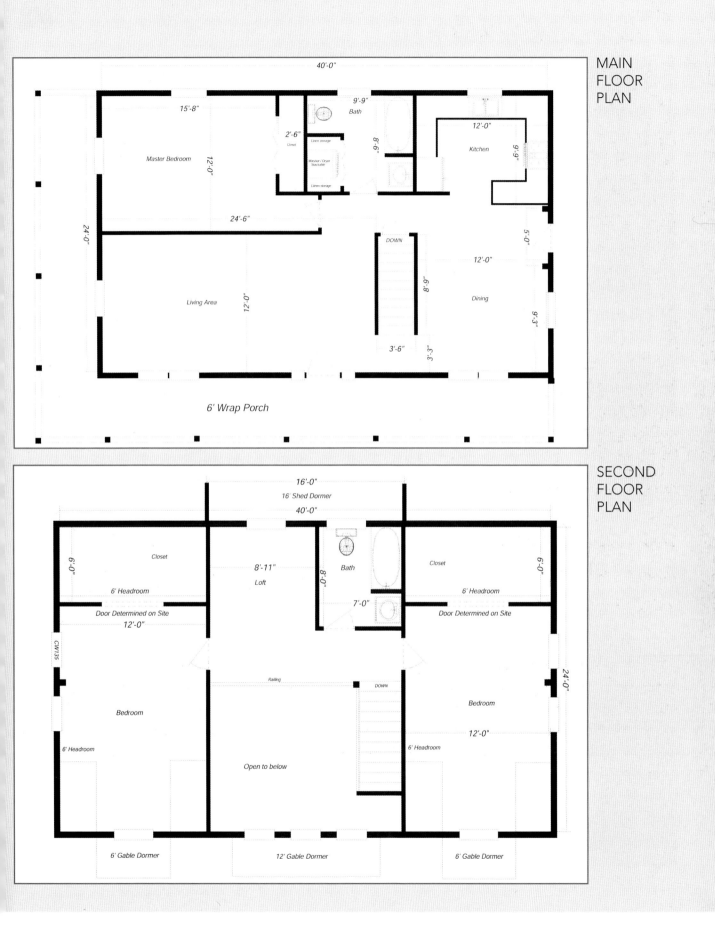

MAIN FLOOR PLAN

40'-0"

15'-8"

9'-9"
Bath

12'-0"

2'-6"
Closet

Kitchen

Linen storage

Washer / Dryer
Stackable

Master Bedroom

12'-0"

9'-8"

9'-9"

Linen storage

24'-6"

24'-0"

DOWN

5'-0"

12'-0"

8'-9"

Living Area

12'-0"

Dining

9'-3"

3'-6"

3'-3"

6' Wrap Porch

16'-0"

16' Shed Dormer

40'-0"

Closet

6'-0"

8'-11"
Loft

Bath

Closet

6'-0"

6' Headroom

8'-0"

6' Headroom

Door Determined on Site

7'-0"

Door Determined on Site

12'-0"

CW135

Railing

DOWN

24'-0"

Bedroom

Bedroom

6' Headroom

6' Headroom

12'-0"

Open to below

6' Gable Dormer

12' Gable Dormer

6' Gable Dormer

The Ledgewood

Three gable dormers in front and a shed dormer out back vary the roofline.

The wrap-around porch of The Ledgewood extends the roofline well past and over the walls.

The Brookview

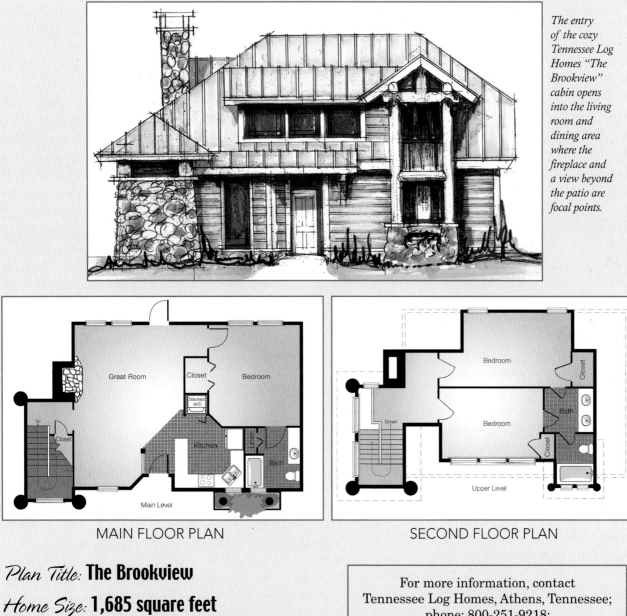

The entry of the cozy Tennessee Log Homes "The Brookview" cabin opens into the living room and dining area where the fireplace and a view beyond the patio are focal points.

MAIN FLOOR PLAN

SECOND FLOOR PLAN

Plan Title: The Brookview

Home Size: 1,685 square feet

Plan Designer: Tennessee Log Homes

For more information, contact
Tennessee Log Homes, Athens, Tennessee;
phone: 800-251-9218;
website: www.tnloghomes.com.

The entry of this cozy cabin opens into the living room and dining area where the fireplace and a view beyond the patio are focal points. The sizable master bedroom's entrance, convenient to the patio, is hidden at the end of the living room.

At the staircase off the dining area is a wrap-around clerestory window, allowing the balcony above to enjoy a 270-degree view. A large hall opens into the twin bedrooms, each of which accesses the Jack and Jill bath. Small walk-in closets serve guests who occupy the rooms or provide supplementary storage space.

Tegeler

A sunroom, grill deck, screened porch, studio and custom-designed windows are some of the added bonuses of the Tegeler log home from Kuhns Bros.

Plan Title: Tegeler (An addition to a log home)

Home Size: 1,350 square feet

Plan Designer: Kuhns Bros. Log Homes

For more information, contact
Kuhns Bros. Log Homes, Lewisburg, Pennsylvania;
phone: 800-326-9614;
website: www.kuhnsbros.com.

This two-story addition comprises all the features of a small home except bedrooms and baths. The highlight is the living room, which is where it connects with the original house. The living room leads to a screened porch with a grill deck that is in convenient proximity to a roomy kitchen with a center island for dining.

Beyond the stairs is a sunroom, above which is a loft studio. A walkway spanning the space above the great room leads to an open loft area with access to a deck. The plan also includes a garage.

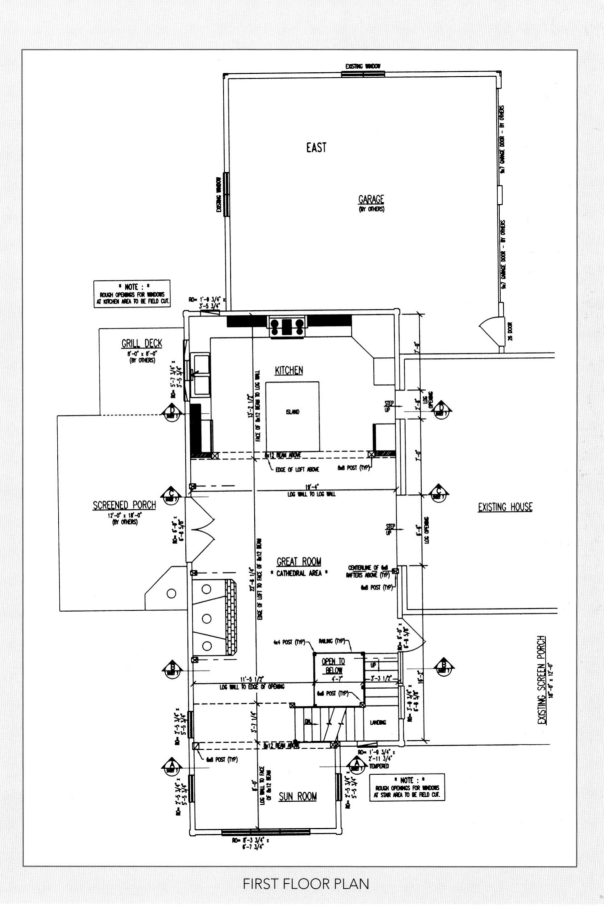

FIRST FLOOR PLAN

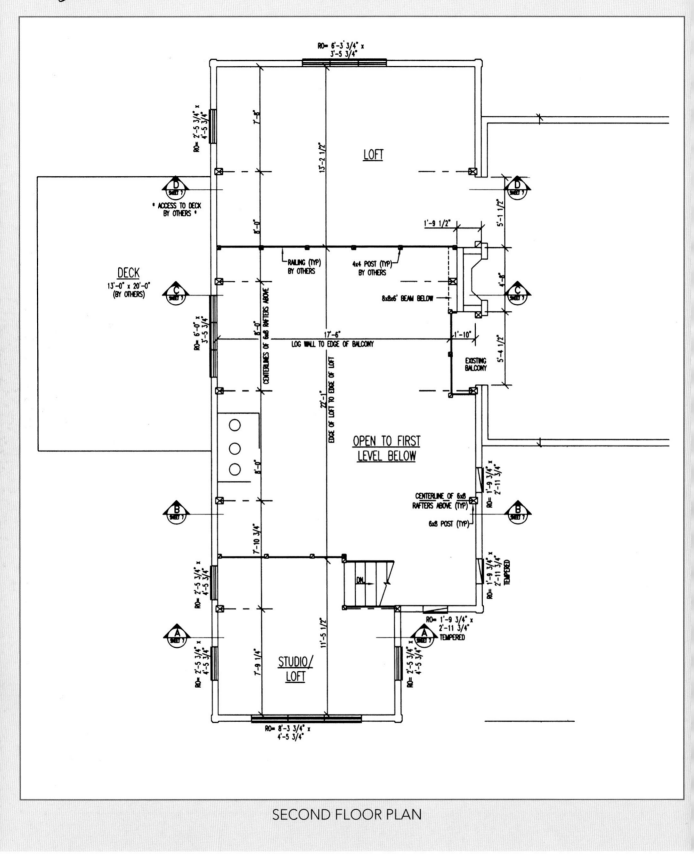

SECOND FLOOR PLAN

The highlight of the Tegeler log home addition is the living room, which is where it connects with an original house.

The roomy kitchen features a center island for dining.

The living room leads to a screened porch with a grill deck.

The Townsend

From the front porch that enters into the living room to the loft and the guest suite in the basement, The Townsend is a cozy home with room to roam.

Plan Title: **The Townsend**

Home Size: **1,348 square feet**

Plan Designer: **Hearthstone**

For more information, contact Hearthstone, Dandridge, Tennessee; phone: 800-247-4442; website: www.hearthstonehomes.com.

This cozy layout gains additional living space outdoors, courtesy of the full-length screened porch on the back of the house, which is accessible from the dining area and master suite, and a front porch that opens to the living room.

The interior space is split into thirds: the master suite, the living room and the kitchen-dining area. Stairs at the back of the living room descend to the basement, which features a guest suite. An open loft overlooks the dining area, living room and master bedroom.

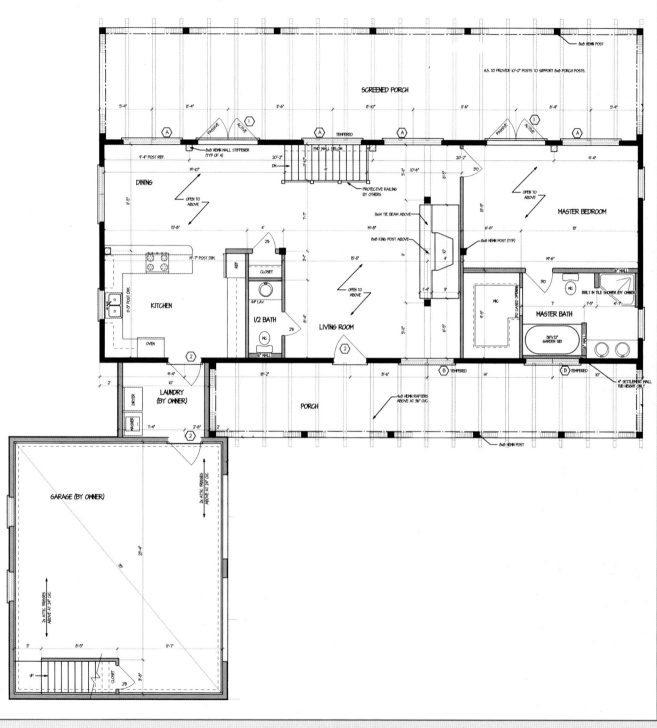

MAIN FLOOR PLAN

The Townsend

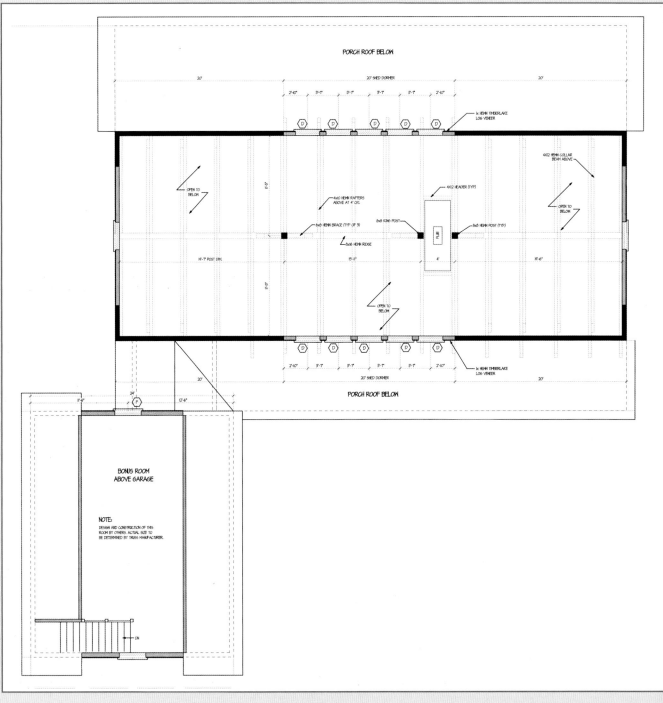

LOFT PLAN

Split into thirds, the interior of The Townsend includes the master suite, the kitchen-dining area (shown) and the living room.

Though a 1,348-square-foot home, the living room of the Townsend is sizeable and comfortable.

The front porch of the Hearthstone Townsend model extends the length of the house.

This cozy layout gains additional living space outdoors, courtesy of the full-length screened porch on the back of the house.

Weekender

Aptly named the "Weekender," the Hearthstone model is a cozy and comfortable cabin built with a Bob Timberlake® profile. The Bob Timberlake style offers logs up to 24 feet in length and follows the natural contour of the log, with heights ranging from 14 to 24 feet.

Plan Title: **Weekender**

Home Size: **668 square feet**

Plan Designer: **Hearthstone**

For more information, contact
Hearthstone, Dandridge, Tennessee;
phone: 800-247-4442;
website: www.hearthstonehomes.com.

This aptly named plan offers a snug sleeping loft, and, on the main level, a kitchen, dining area and living room. The master bedroom, a separate bath, laundry and family room are on the lower level. The front porch and rear deck provide a welcome opportunity to extend the living space beyond the walls.

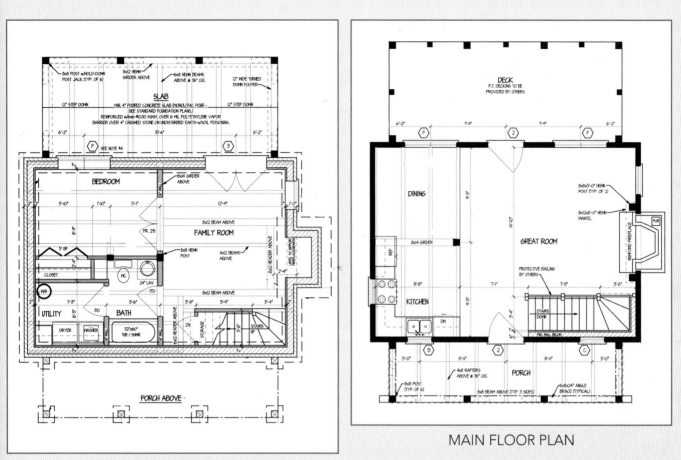

LOWER LEVEL FLOOR PLAN

MAIN FLOOR PLAN

LOFT PLAN

Plans Under 2,000 Square Feet · **53**

Weekender

The main level of the Hearthstone Weekender includes a kitchen, dining area and living room.

A snug sleeping loft overlooks the rest of the Weekender cabin.

A front porch, back deck and patio under the deck (shown) extend the living space beyond the walls.

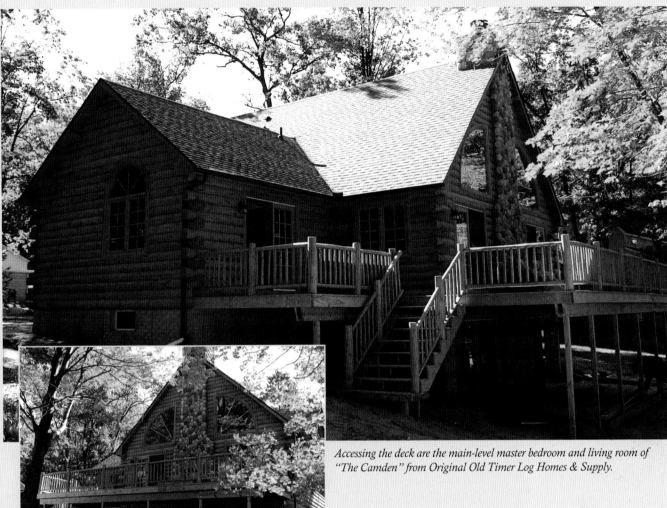

Accessing the deck are the main-level master bedroom and living room of "The Camden" from Original Old Timer Log Homes & Supply.

Plan Title: **The Camden**

Home Size: **1,973 square feet**

Plan Designer:

Original Old Timer Log Homes & Supply

For more information, contact
Original Old Timer Log Homes & Supply, Mount
Juliet, Tennessee;
phone: 800-467-3006;
website: www.oldtimerloghomes.com.

This compact plan is noteworthy for providing two master suites, one on the main level, the other occupying the loft. A third bedroom is located behind the stairs.

The galley-style kitchen leads to a generous utility room. The main-level master bedroom and the living room access the deck. Living and dining rooms are open above with exposed beam trusses, while the kitchen and bedrooms have cozy, beamed ceilings. Fan-shaped windows in the gable add to the home's beauty.

The Camden

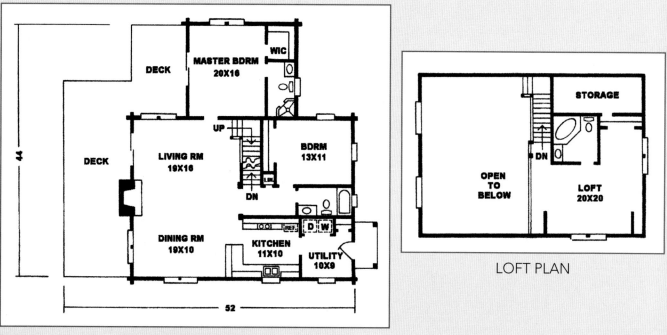

MAIN FLOOR PLAN

LOFT PLAN

The Camden's living and dining rooms are open above with exposed beam trusses.

The kitchen of the Camden is galley style with a beamed ceiling.

The cozy Camden plan is noteworthy for providing two master suites, one on the main level and the other in the loft.

The Rutherford

Despite its cozy size, the Old Timer Log Homes & Supply "The Rutherford" model showcases a wraparound, covered porch, a spacious deck and prominent gable windows.

Plan Title: **The Rutherford**

Home Size: **1,749 square feet**

Plan Designer: **Original Old Timer Log Homes & Supply**

> For more information, contact Original Old Timer Log Homes & Supply,
> Mount Juliet, Tennessee; phone: 800-467-3006;
> website: www.oldtimerloghomes.com.

Despite its cozy size, the plan's wrap-around covered porch, spacious deck and prominent gable windows enlarge its appearance. It features an open living room, dining area and kitchen. Situating the fireplace in the corner of the living room allows an unobstructed view.

A large utility room is across the hall from a small bedroom. The master suite, with sizable walk-in closet and bathroom that includes a corner tub, occupies the loft, which overlooks the great room. A large island for dining defines the kitchen boundary.

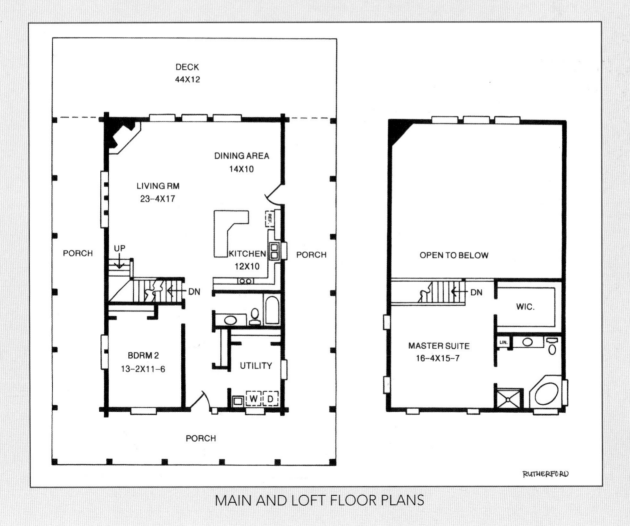

MAIN AND LOFT FLOOR PLANS

The Rutherford

The combination living room, dining area and kitchen of "The Rutherford" gives it an open, airy feel.

A large island for dining defines the kitchen boundary.

Depending on where one plans to build "The Rutherford," the view through the gable windows could be spectacular.

The master suite, with sizable walk-in closet and bathroom that includes a corner tub, occupies the loft, which overlooks the great room.

Tomahawk

The expansive front porch and deck of the Strongwood Log Home Company "Tomahawk" add dimension and afford plenty of opportunity for outdoor living, while walls of windows shed light on the interior.

Plan Title: **Tomahawk**

Home Size: **1,940 square feet**

Plan Designer: **Strongwood Log Home Company**

For more, contact
Strongwood Log Home Co.,
Waupaca, Wisconsin;
phone: 866-258-4818;
website: www.strongwoodloghome.com.

The efficient chalet layout incorporates two bedrooms on the main level, an ideal arrangement for children or company, while providing privacy upstairs for the master bedroom and a small sitting loft.

The cathedral ceiling enhances the openness of the great room, and the expansive front porch and deck add dimension and afford plenty of opportunity for outdoor living. An eat-at counter defines the kitchen space, which takes in views of the outdoors and fireplace.

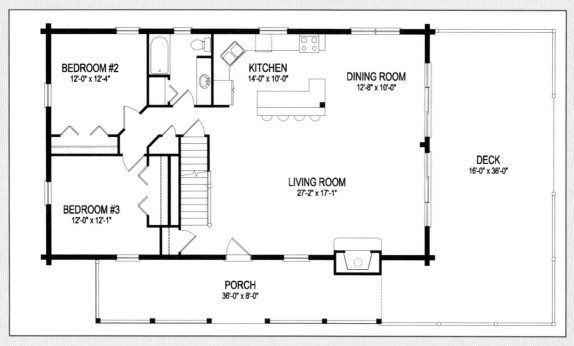

MAIN FLOOR PLAN

SECOND FLOOR PLAN

Tomahawk

The "Tomahawk's" cathedral ceiling enhances the openness of the great room. Shown are the great rooms of two "Tomahawk" homes customized to customer specifications.

A dining counter defines the kitchen space, and a small sitting loft overlooks it, the dining room, fireplace and outdoors.

The dormers and covered porches of the Katahdin Cedar Log Homes "Sebec" add visual appeal, while a "bumped out" lower level makes room for a dining room on one side of the living room and a bedroom on the other.

Plan Title: **Sebec**

Home Size: **1,429 square feet**

Plan Designer: **Katahdin Cedar Log Homes**

For more, contact
Katahdin Cedar Log Homes, Oakfield, Maine;
phone: 800-845-4533;
website: www.katahdincedarloghomes.com.

A staggered layout makes this small plan seem larger by bumping out the lower level for a dining room on one side of the living room and a bedroom on the other. A generous, open kitchen is designed around a center island.

A cathedral ceiling makes the spacious living room feel even more open. A large open loft adjoins a second bedroom and bath. Dormers and covered porches add visual appeal.

Sebec

Porch
21'0"x6'0"

Porch
20'6"6'0"

Bath

Clo.
Clo.

Kitchen
10'8"x13'8"

Pan.

Lin.

Bedroom
11'9"x19'5"

Dining Room
7'9"x15'5"

Living Room
19'10"x15'8"

Porch
12'0"x8'0"

15'-0"

16'-0"

3'-0"

4'-0"

20'-0"

34'-0"

10'-0"

8'-0"

20'-0"

12'-0"

40'-0"

MAIN FLOOR PLAN

Storage

Storage

Open Loft
12'8"x13'8"

Bath

Storage

Storage

Clo.

Bedroom
12'0"x15'8"

Storage

Cathedral Ceiling

Sto.

Sto.

34'-0"

32'-0"

LOFT PLAN

A cathedral ceiling makes the spacious living room of the Katahdin Cedar Log Homes "Sebec" model feel even more open.

A generous, open kitchen is designed around a center island.

A large open loft adjoins an upstairs bedroom and bath.

The Belmont

Three dormers vary the roofline of the StoneMill Log Homes "The Belmont."

Plan Title: **The Belmont**

Home Size: **1,366 square feet**

Plan Designer: **StoneMill Log Homes**

For more, contact
StoneMill Log Homes, Knoxville, Tennessee; phone:
800-438-8274;
website: www.stonemill.com.

This compact layout accommodates a full-scale great room on the main level, with a cathedral ceiling topping the living and dining areas, and two bedrooms. The larger bedroom enjoys access to the front porch.

Upstairs, three dormers vary the roofline, one of which adds interior headroom for the small sitting loft over the kitchen, and a second benefiting a bedroom with its own bath and a large walk-in closet. A rear porch extends the living space outside.

The largest bedroom of "The Belmont" from StoneMill Log Homes enjoys access to the front porch.

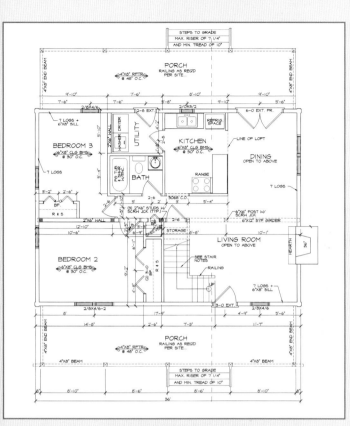

MAIN FLOOR PLAN

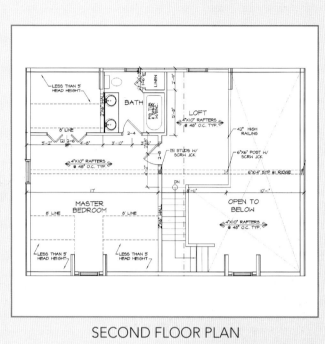

SECOND FLOOR PLAN

A cathedral ceiling tops the living and dining areas, and two bedrooms.

Not Too Big, Not Too Small

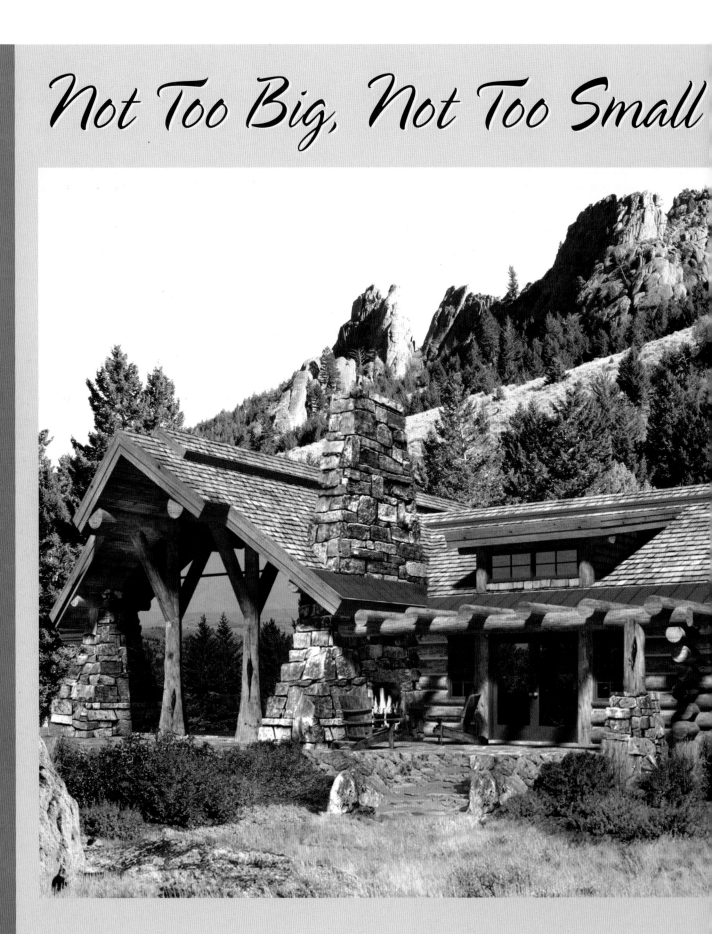

Log homes showcased in this section range in size from between 2,000 and 4,000 total square feet

People contemplating log-home design usually worry way too much about arranging the rooms, when they should address broader concerns. The impetus for any design is as much philosophical as it is practical.

This doesn't mean enrolling in graduate school before you may declare that your master bedroom ought to be on the first floor, not the second. But at least be able to express what it is about log homes that inspires you to live in one.

Perhaps your reason is, "Because I have fond memories of spending childhood summers at my family's log cabin beside a lake, and I long to re-create that happy feeling."

Or, "Because I want a house that is both strong and beautiful."

Or, "Because I've accumulated lots of money, and I want to spend it on a home that will make others envy my success."

There are practical, fanciful, even foolish reasons why people choose to live in log homes. All are valid.

Whatever draws you to a log home will reveal itself in the design. If you want your home to be a showplace, it will boast expansive rooms with sweeping views, towering fireplaces and fancy fixtures. If you envision togetherness, you'll seek cozy spaces for gathering. If you long to feel part of the great outdoors, you'll enjoy windows, porches and decks, perhaps a sunroom.

Before listing specific features, spend time thinking about what a house is, and what you want your house to be.

The architect Witold Rybczynski identifies several notions in his 1986 book, *Home: A Short History of an Idea*. They are nostalgia, intimacy and privacy, domesticity, commodity and delight, ease, light and air, efficiency, style and substance, austerity and comfort, and well-being. All come into play, to varying degrees, when you are wondering whether the kitchen should be to the left of the dining room or how close your children's rooms should be to the master bedroom.

Another helpful book is Akiko Busch's *Geography of Home: Writings on Where We Live*. A home, the author points out, is far more than four walls and a roof. It contains our private and public lives, our families, our memories and aspirations, and reflects our attitudes toward society, culture, the environment and our neighbors.

Underlying both books is the idea of comfort. Whatever or whoever you have to be when you are outside your home, while you are within its walls, you can be yourself. A home should promote and protect this sense of self. You should feel comfortable. How you achieve that comfort is the aim of design.

When you talk to architects and builders, the materials that make a house may easily distract you. When you listen to yourself, you discover the spiritual ingredients that make a house a home.

Understand what these are. Then, and only then, pick up your pencil and begin sketching room layouts. The result will be a house you can live with, as well as a home you can live in.

The Atkins

A second story with a generous loft area gives The Atkins model from Northeastern Log Homes a height advantage over other log homes.

Plan Title: **The Atkins**

Home Size: **3,426 square feet**

Plan Designer: **Northeastern Log Homes**

For more, contact
Northeastern Log Homes, Kenduskeag, Maine;
phone: 800-624-2797;
website: www.northeasternlog.com.

This efficient, semi-open layout enters via an ample hallway to sudden openness to a tall living room, achieved with a second story that has a generous loft area. The height of the living room allows natural light and views through floor-to-ceiling windows looking out at the wide, rear deck.

The living and dining spaces share an open-hearth central fireplace. The roomy loft accommodates many uses, besides acting as a bridge between two wings. One wing features a bedroom with its own bath, and on the second wing, two bedrooms, each with its own balcony, share a bath.

The height of the living room allows natural light and views through floor-to-ceiling windows looking out at the wide rear deck.

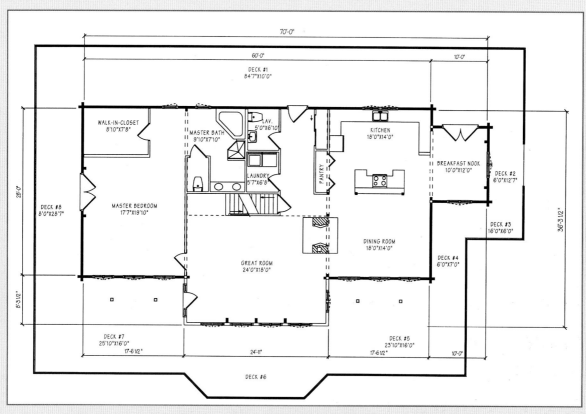

MAIN FLOOR PLAN

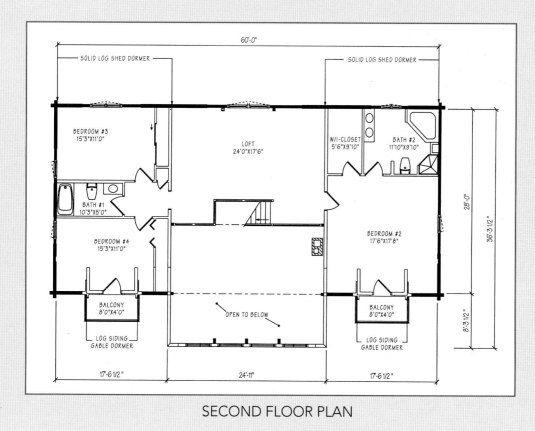

SECOND FLOOR PLAN

The Naville

A deck and multiple porches broaden the living space of "The Naville" from Northeastern Log Homes.

Plan Title: The Naville

Home Size: 3,200 square feet

Plan Designer: Northeastern Log Homes

For more, contact
Northeastern Log Homes, Kenduskeag, Maine;
phone: 800-624-2797;
website: www.northeasternlog.com.

Multiple porches and a deck broaden this home's usable living space. An attached, solid-log garage accesses the entryway on the main level, keeps the layout symmetrical and underlies two bedrooms. The garage is well away from the lower-level master suite, a private enclave that enjoys roominess and direct access to the deck.

The master bedroom shares a fireplace with the living room. The U-shaped kitchen opens across an island to the living area and is flanked by a generous pantry and a utility room.

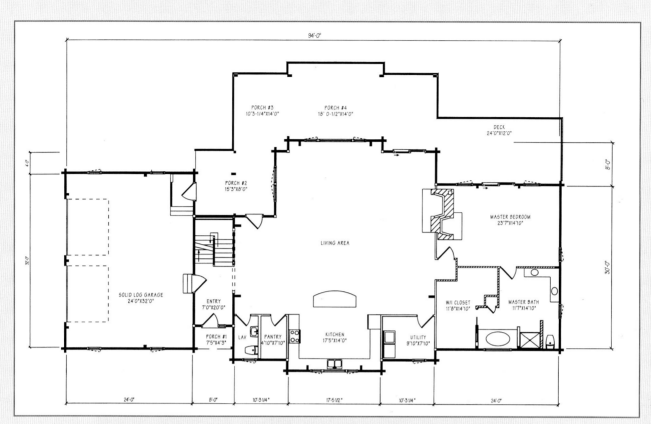

MAIN FLOOR PLAN

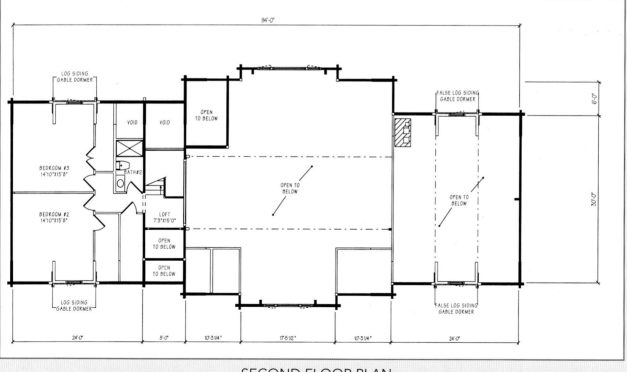

SECOND FLOOR PLAN

The Naville

Imagine dining in this high-ceilinged room with fantastic view and magnificent interior woodwork and design.

The master bedroom shares a fireplace with the living room.

The master suite enjoys direct access to the deck.

The exterior of the Northeastern Log Homes "The Westfield" retains the traditional full-length farmer front porch, but its dormers, breezeway and roofline add contemporary styling.

Plan Title: The Westfield

Home Size: 2,100 square feet

Plan Designer: Northeastern Log Homes

For more, contact
Northeastern Log Homes,
Kenduskeag, Maine; phone: 800-624-2797;
website: www.northeasternlog.com.

The exterior retains the traditional full-length farmer front porch, but its dormers, breezeway and roofline add contemporary styling. Inside, it features a half-cathedral ceiling over a formal living room, while above, a corner loft suggests a variety of uses.

Two upstairs bedrooms share an interior balcony overlooking the long living room. To conserve space, the stairs are located at the entry and against the wall. A small deck off the eat-in kitchen makes the home seem even roomier, and the front deck ties the breezeway into the home.

The Westfield

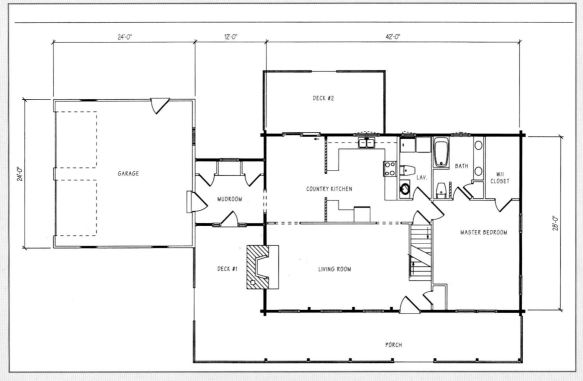

MAIN FLOOR PLAN

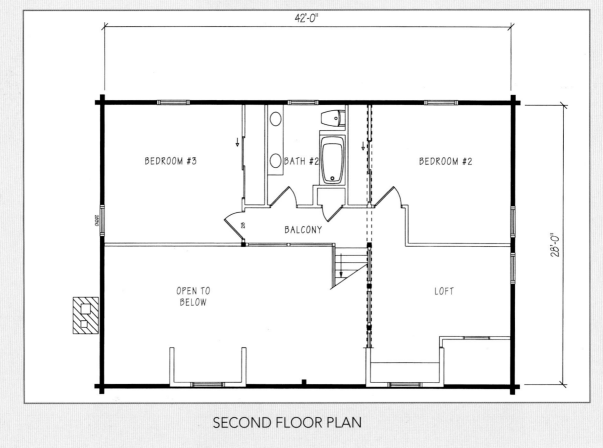

SECOND FLOOR PLAN

An eat-in kitchen is cozy, but a small deck off the kitchen makes the home seem even roomier than it is.

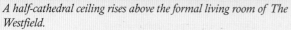

A half-cathedral ceiling rises above the formal living room of The Westfield.

The dormer makes for a cozy place to lay back and relax.

Two upstairs bedrooms share an interior balcony overlooking the long living room.

Timberlake

Several features, like windows, a cathedral ceiling, an 8-foot bump out and a garage in which logs, not garage doors, show from the front define the Cedarcraft Log Homes "Timberlake" model.

Plan Title: Timberlake

Home Size: 2,884 square feet

Plan Designer: Cedarcraft Log Homes

For more information, contact
Cedarcraft Log Homes, Concord, Ohio;
phone: 800-982-2902;
website:www.cedarcraftloghomes.com

Windows, a cathedral ceiling and an 8-foot bump out distinguish the central living room of the Cedarcraft Log Homes "Timberlake." Bonus space comes from a loft over the kitchen and dining area, with both rooms located behind a wide fireplace and stairs.

All three bedrooms and two baths are off the living room, with the master suite accessing the sunroom and, through it, the deck that connects to the dining area. A cozy den lies off a hallway leading from the rest of the house to the garage, which is turned to show logs, not garage doors, and balances the bedroom wing.

MAIN FLOOR PLAN

Flanked by log corners, the porch of the Cedarcraft Log Homes "Hudson" is set back under soaring windows to provide a dramatic entry.

Plan Title: **Hudson**

Home Size: **2,540 square feet**

Plan Designer: **Cedarcraft Log Homes**

For more information, contact
Cedarcraft Log Homes, Concord, Ohio;
phone: 800-982-2902;
website:www.cedarcraftloghomes.com

The porch of the Cedarcraft Log Homes "Hudson," flanked by log corners, is set back under soaring windows to provide a dramatic entry. The real drama, though, is the master suite. Twin walk-in closets and a roomy bathroom combine for more square footage than the bedroom, which by itself is nearly 300 square feet.

The master wing also has a small, second bedroom with bay window. A staggered garage suggests an L-shaped footprint while adding a fifth roofline. A spacious loft (roughly 21-by-20 feet) enjoys light from the front windows.

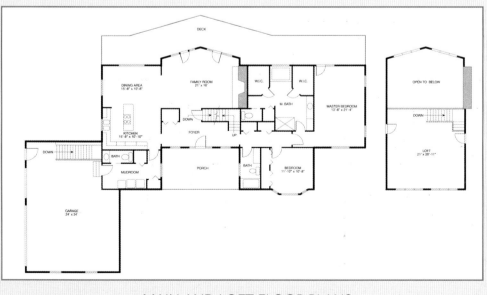

MAIN AND LOFT FLOOR PLANS

The Forge

Adding just two rows of logs raises the first-floor ceiling height of the Northeastern Log Homes "The Forge," making the loft roomier.

Plan Title: **The Forge**

Home Size: **2,022 square feet**

Plan Designer: **Northeastern Log Homes**

For more, contact
Northeastern Log Homes, Kenduskeag, Maine;
phone: 800-624-2797;
website: www.northeasternlog.com.

This compact plan creates spaciousness while still partitioning rooms for privacy. The loft is the key. Adding just two rows of logs raises the first-floor ceiling height and makes the loft roomier, eliminating the need for bedroom dormers. It also raises the porch roof to let in more sunlight.

A first-floor master suite leads to an ample spa and a private deck. The efficient kitchen, which also accesses a wide deck, is ideal for informal meals, from breakfast to barbecues.

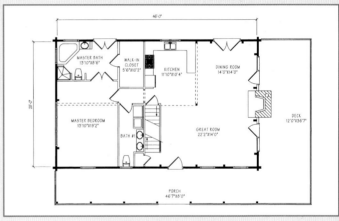

MAIN FLOOR PLAN

SECOND FLOOR PLAN

The raised ceiling of the first floor makes the great room all that much greater.

The efficient kitchen accesses a wide deck and is ideal for informal meals.

A first-floor master suite leads to an ample spa and private deck.

Concord

Only the deck of the Cedarcraft Log Homes "Concord" projects past the front prow.

Plan Title: **Concord**

Home Size: **3,095 square feet**

Plan Designer: **Cedarcraft Log Homes**

For more information, contact Cedarcraft Log Homes, Concord, Ohio; phone: 800-982-2902; website: www.cedarcraftloghomes.com

A full front prow of the Cedarcraft Log Homes "Concord" gives expression to an open great room ringed by the master suite and various storage and utility compartments. Included is a hallway off the kitchen leading to the out-of-the-way but still-attached garage.

The master bedroom opens to the front porch, which becomes a deck projecting ahead of the prow. Atop the master bedroom is a second bedroom connected by a loft. The loft, in turn, overlooks the living room, and leads into a den with its own stairs. The stairs descend into the kitchen, mudroom and garage.

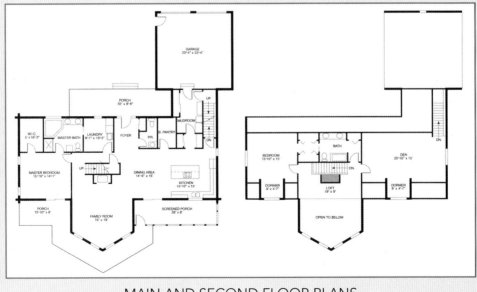

MAIN AND SECOND FLOOR PLANS

Dormers on the upper level of the otherwise horizontal "Auburn" relieve a long roofline.

Plan Title: **Auburn**

Home Size: **2,765 square feet**

Plan Designer: **Cedarcraft Log Homes**

For more information, contact
Cedarcraft Log Homes, Concord, Ohio;
phone: 800-982-2902;
website: www.cedarcraftloghomes.com

The horizontal layout, punctuated by the 35-foot-wide garage, devotes one first-floor wing to a spread-out master bedroom suite. The master suite opens to a handy den, which accesses the full-front porch.

The great room comprises not just the living room, dining area and kitchen, but also a large family room leading to both the kitchen and a back porch. The upper level uses dormers to enlarge two bedrooms, connected by a loft, and for relief from the long roofline.

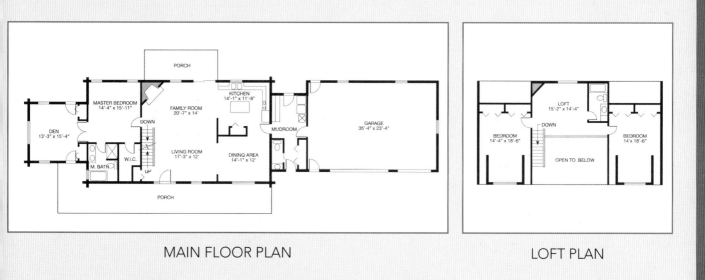

MAIN FLOOR PLAN

LOFT PLAN

Madison

Plan Title: **Madison**

Home Size: **2,990 square feet**

Plan Designer:

Cedarcraft Log Homes

For more information, contact
Cedarcraft Log Homes,
Concord, Ohio;
phone: 800-982-2902;
website: www.cedarcraftloghomes.com

This layout is configured to take full advantage of a front view, featuring plenty of windows, especially in the uplifting great room. Flanking the spacious great room, with its central fireplace, are the master suite and, on the opposite side, an ample laundry room and den. The master suite accesses its own porch and the bathroom accommodates a two-person whirlpool tub.

The second story contains a big loft, which overlooks the living room and shares the view, as well as three bedrooms and a bath.

MAIN AND SECOND FLOOR PLANS

Plan Title: **Keen**

Home Size: **3,865 square feet**

Plan Designer: **Log Homes of America**

For more information, contact
Log Homes of America,
Banner Elk, North Carolina;
phone: 828-963-7777;
website: www.loghomesofamerica.com.

Natural light flows through this open layout, courtesy of the great room's oversized windows. A well-defined entry leads to the dining area, which exhibits a low ceiling that extends to the adjacent kitchen and library. The kitchen and library ring the two-story great room.

Outside, twin dormers echo the peak of the great room roof, while inside they enlarge two mini suites. The high point is the spacious master suite, which shares the interior fireplace with the great room. A 10-foot-deep deck and side porch bring the living space outdoors.

Keen

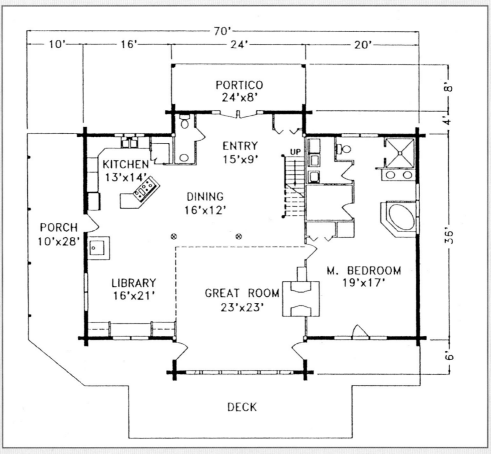

MAIN FLOOR PLAN

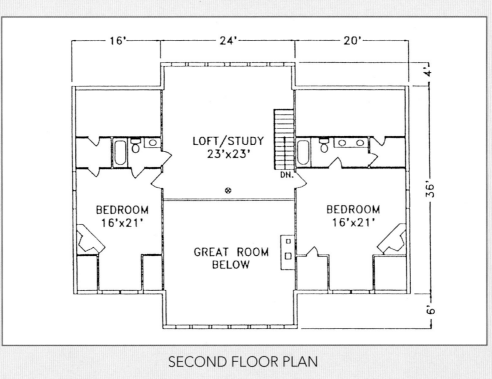

SECOND FLOOR PLAN

The fireplace in the great room is shared on the other side of the wall with a spacious master suite.

Dogwood II

The two porches and deck extend the living space of the "Dogwood II" to the outdoors.

Plan Title: **Dogwood II**

Home Size: **2,468 square feet**

Plan Designer: **Appalachian Log Structures**

For more information, contact
Appalachian Log Structures,
Ripley, West Virginia; phone: 800-458-9990;
website: www.applog.com.

The layout of the Appalachian Log Structures "Dogwood II" is designed to extend the home's living space to the outdoors, with two easily accessible porches and a deck.

A compact great room uses the loft and fireplace to define the kitchen space. A bonus feature is a den, bumped out to separate it from the rest of the house and convenient to the powder room, making it perfect for a home office. Over it is the larger of the upstairs bedrooms. The loft overlooks the living room and dining area.

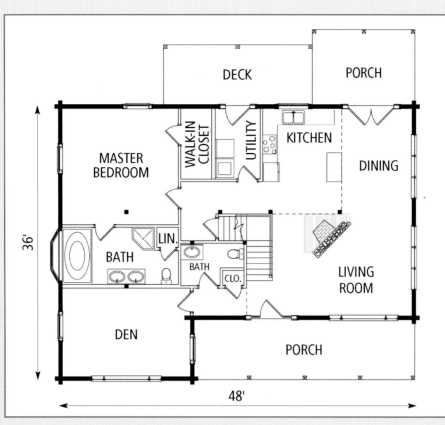

FIRST FLOOR PLAN

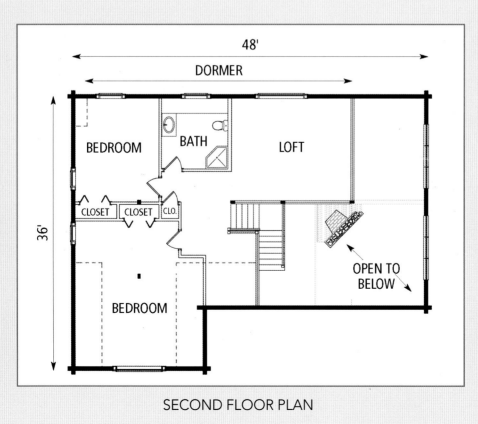

SECOND FLOOR PLAN

Fair Oaks

Three dormers make up the aesthetic standouts of the "Fair Oaks" model from Appalachian Log Structures. A wrap-around porch and extended roofline also deserve mention.

Plan Title: **Fair Oaks**

Home Size: **2,084 square feet**

Plan Designer: **Appalachian Log Structures**

For more information, contact Appalachian Log Structures, Ripley, West Virginia; phone: 800-458-9990; website: www.applog.com.

Triple dormers and a full-length front porch add prominence to the facade of this home. Laid out efficiently, it uses stairs and the rear wall of the master bedroom closet, for instance, to carve a foyer out of otherwise open space.

The foyer and adjacent powder and laundry room interrupt the flow between the dining and living rooms, while the L-shaped kitchen opens to both. A narrow loft divides the upper-level twin bedrooms and baths.

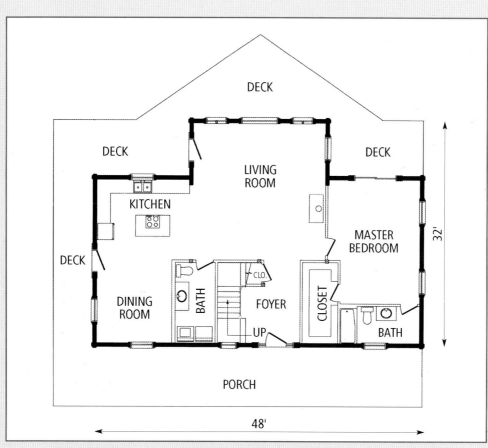

MAIN FLOOR PLAN

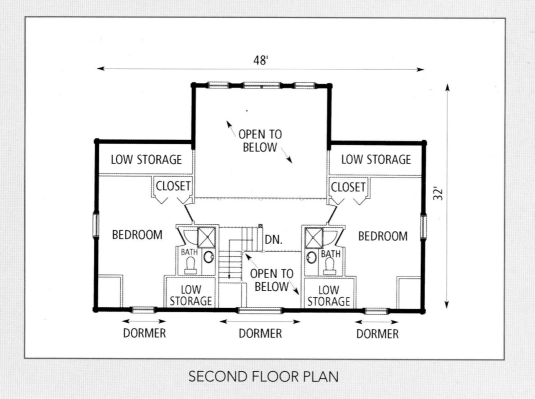

SECOND FLOOR PLAN

Stoneridge

The majestic entry of the Appalachian Log Structures "Stoneridge" is complements of a large dormer and gabled porch.

Plan Title: **Stoneridge**

Home Size: **2,028 square feet**

Plan Designer: **Appalachian Log Structures**

For more information, contact
Appalachian Log Structures,
Ripley, West Virginia; phone: 800-458-9990;
website: www.applog.com.

A large dormer and gabled porch provide a majestic entry to this home with a compartmentalized plan that accommodates three bedrooms and 2 1/2 baths. Exposed timber-frame rafters highlight the living room and dining room, which open onto a rear deck. Off the living room, an outdoor fireplace extends enjoyment of the screened porch from early spring to late fall.

The first-floor master suite features a fireplace and large walk-in closet. Upstairs, two bedrooms and a family room leave open space over not just the living room, but also the dining room.

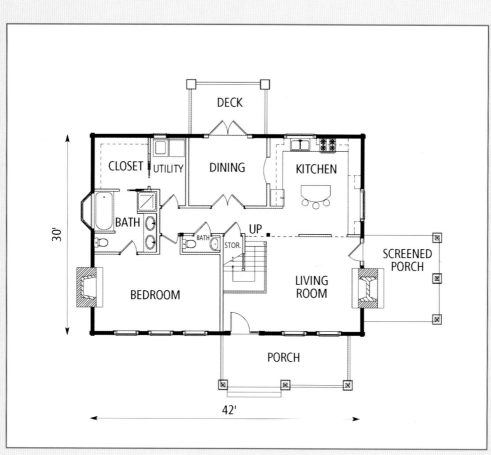

MAIN FLOOR PLAN

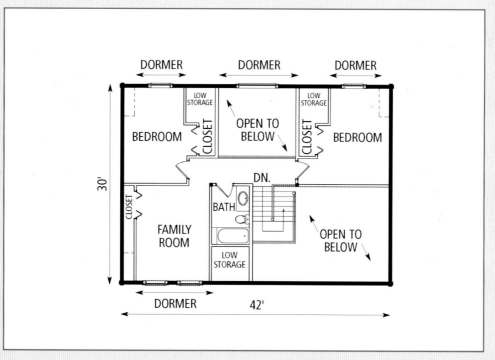

SECOND FLOOR PLAN

Park Vista

With plenty of glass, the Log Homes of America "Park Vista" model combines classic log and heavy timber construction.

Plan Title: **Park Vista**

Home Size: **2,774 square feet**

Plan Designer: **Log Homes of America**

For more information, contact
Log Homes of America, Banner Elk, North Carolina;
phone: 828-963-7777;
website: www.loghomesofamerica.com.

This plan combines classic log and heavy timber construction, with plenty of glass. The modified L-shaped kitchen is tucked beneath the loft, which overlooks the dining and living rooms.

The roomy master suite forms a private wing that opens onto the expansive deck and is convenient to the laundry room. A second main-floor bedroom lies behind the stairs. Above it, the third bedroom has the loft all to itself, with its own bathroom.

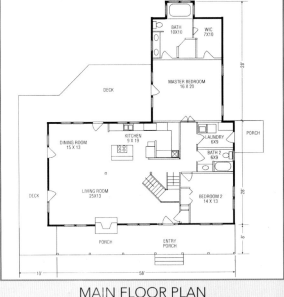

MAIN FLOOR PLAN

SECOND FLOOR PLAN

The Grandview

The front entry, beside the two-car garage, leads directly into the living room.

The wraparound porch of "The Grandview," a modified chalet-style house from Coventry Log Homes, adds living space that is especially conducive to entertaining large groups.

Plan Title: **The Grandview**

Home Size: **2,704 square feet**

Plan Designer: **Coventry Log Homes**

For more information, contact
Coventry Log Homes,
Woodsville, New Hampshire;
phone: 800-308-7505;
website: www.coventryloghomes.com.

This modified chalet-style plan includes a wraparound porch to add living space that is especially conducive to entertaining larger groups. The front entry, beside the two-car garage, leads directly into the living room, which opens to the kitchen and dining room.

A cathedral ceiling tops the living and dining areas, while the first-floor master suite enjoys privacy. Upstairs, two bedrooms and a full bath adjoin open loft space overlooking the lower level and benefiting from light through the living room's wall-top windows.

The Grandview

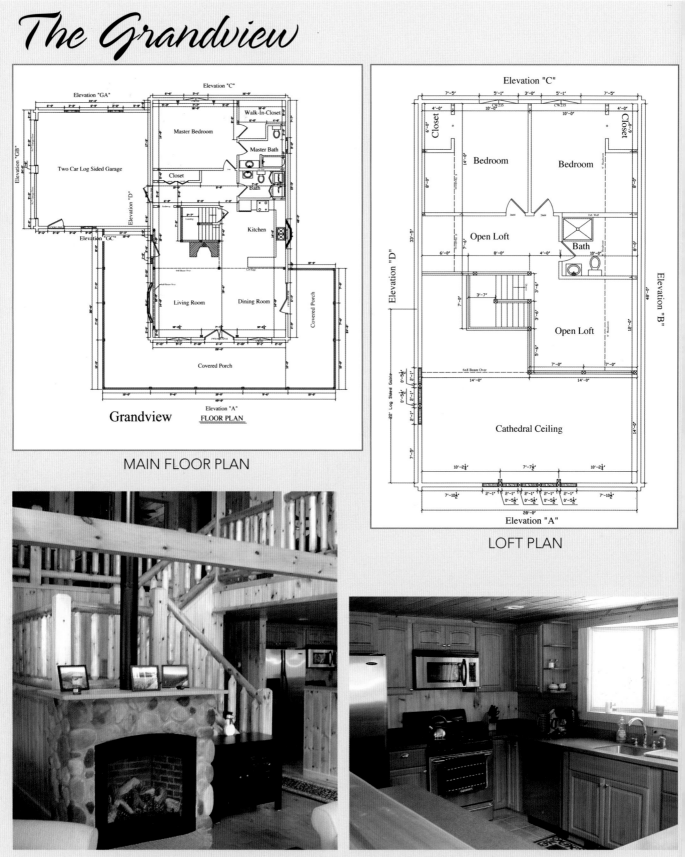

MAIN FLOOR PLAN

Grandview

Elevation "A"
FLOOR PLAN

LOFT PLAN

The living room enters into the kitchen, which is partitioned with half walls.

A cathedral ceiling tops the living and dining areas of The Grandview.

The Kinsman

The wraparound deck is a defining feature of Coventry Log Homes' "The Kinsman," as is the deep, covered porch on one side.

Plan Title: **The Kinsman**

Home Size: **2,013 square feet**

Plan Designer: **Coventry Log Homes**

For more information, contact
Coventry Log Homes,
Woodsville, New Hampshire;
phone: 800-308-7505;
website: www.coventryloghomes.com.

A deep covered porch and wide sun deck broaden the lines of this home, and the lower level enjoys openness in the great room. That space adjoins a private master suite with a 40-square-foot walk-in closet.

The second floor features a small loft sitting area serving two bedrooms, one of which enjoys a roomy closet and a bonus alcove that gains headroom from the shed dormer. The same dormer enlarges the smaller bedroom and the bath.

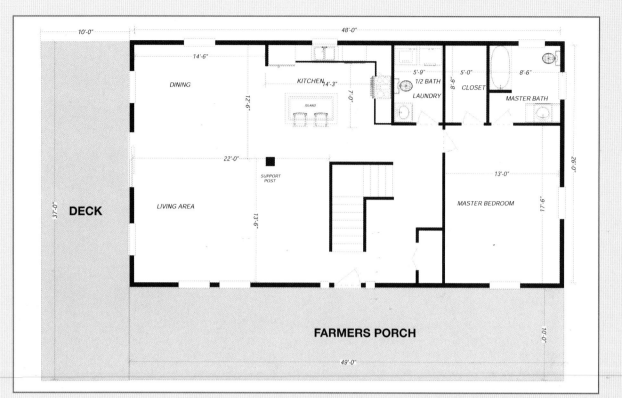

MAIN FLOOR PLAN

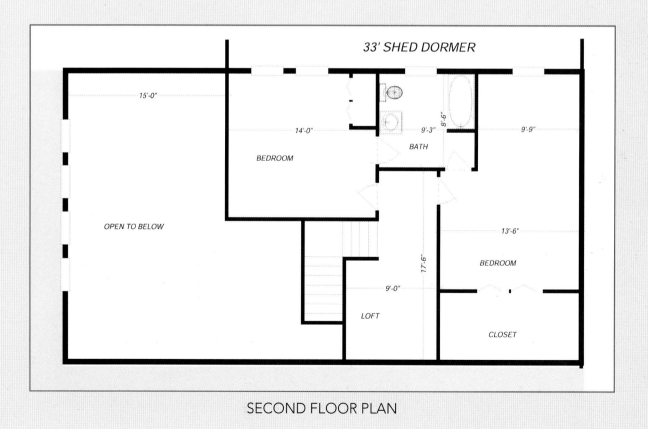

SECOND FLOOR PLAN

Like a great many modern log homes, the great room of "The Kinsman" benefits from an open design concept and leads into the kitchen.

The covered entry of the Alpine Log Homes "Cozy Cove" adds drama to the overall design of the structure.

The Cozy Cove plan relies on outdoor spaces, including a wide, welcoming deck spanning the rear of the home.

Plan Title: **Cozy Cove**

Home Size: **3,189 square feet**

Plan Designer: **Alpine Log Homes**

For more information, contact
Alpine Log Homes, Victor, Montana;
phone: 406-642-3451;
website: www.alpineloghomes.com.

This plan relies on outdoor spaces, including a wide, welcoming deck spanning the rear of the home and a side screened porch adjacent to the dining room. The covered entry adds drama and leads to the foyer, which serves as a transition space. The master suite is tucked away off the great room. Downstairs are three more bedrooms, two baths, a walkout family room equal in size to the great room above and a spacious storage room below the screened porch.

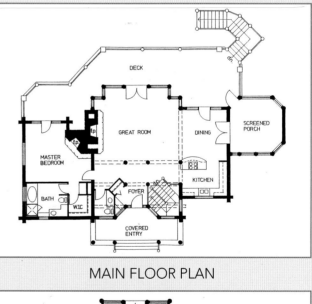

MAIN FLOOR PLAN

LOWER LEVEL FLOOR PLAN

Cumberland

The entry of the Southland Log Homes "Cumberland" leads directly into the great room and sunroom beyond. The bay window houses the luxurious master bath.

Plan Title: **Cumberland**

Home Size: **3,893 square feet**

Plan Designer: **Southland Log Homes**

For more information, contact
Southland Log Homes, Irmo, South Carolina;
phone: 800-828-1492;
website: www.southlandloghomes.com.

Compartmentalizing this layout prevents it from being overcome by vastness. The entry leads directly to the great room and the sunroom beyond. Flanking the long space are two similar arrangements, one containing the breakfast nook, kitchen and formal dining room, the other dedicated to the master suite and a library.

A bay window off the twin walk-in closets houses the luxurious master bath. Upstairs, a balcony over the great room links two mirror image wings, each with two bedrooms and a bath. A wrap-around porch and rear deck offer ample space for outdoor relaxation.

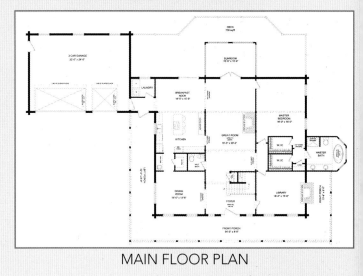

MAIN FLOOR PLAN

SECOND FLOOR PLAN

With five bedrooms and 4 ½ baths, the layout of the Southland Log Homes "Lawrenceburg" is generous, making it ideal for a large family.

Plan Title: **Lawrenceburg**

Home Size: **3,069 square feet**

Plan Designer: **Southland Log Homes**

For more information, contact
Southland Log Homes, Irmo, South Carolina;
phone: 800-828-1492;
website: www.southlandloghomes.com.

This generous layout offers five bedrooms and 4 1/2 baths, plus plenty of storage, making it ideal for a large family. Highlights are a rear porch off the master bedroom, which also features a luxurious master bath and a glass alcove with a custom tub.

A large room with pantry and laundry sits just off the roomy kitchen. A bedroom adjacent to the kitchen could easily serve as a study or home office. Of the three upstairs bedrooms, the one atop the master bedroom is large enough to be a second master suite.

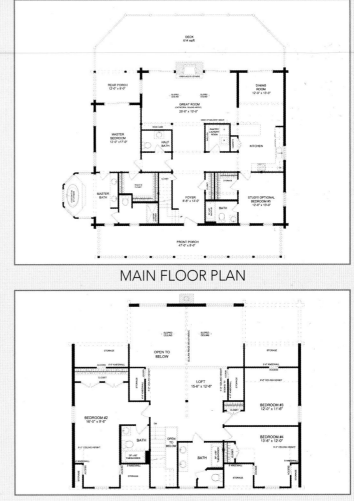

MAIN FLOOR PLAN

SECOND FLOOR PLAN

Seven Gables

The Seven Gables plan from Gastineau Log Homes focuses attention toward the rear of the home, where windows and glass doors allow multiple views and access to a spacious deck.

Plan Title: **Seven Gables**

Home Size: **3,062 square feet**

Plan Designer: **Gastineau Log Homes**

For more information, contact
Gastineau Log Homes, New Bloomfield, Missouri;
phone: 800-654-9253;
website: www.oakloghome.com.

The Seven Gables plan from Gastineau Log Homes focuses attention toward the rear of the home, where windows and glass doors allow multiple views and access to a spacious deck.

The formal entry enjoys a soaring, two-story ceiling, open staircase and view into the loft. The large living room features a central fireplace, cathedral ceiling and a window wall with either circle-top or trapezoid glass. Two upstairs bedrooms, each with a roomy closet, share the open loft and a bathroom with shower stall.

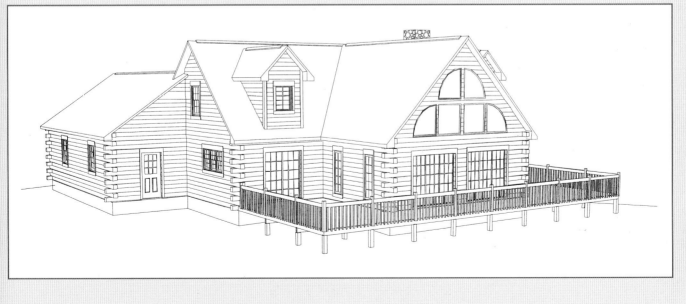

Seven Gables

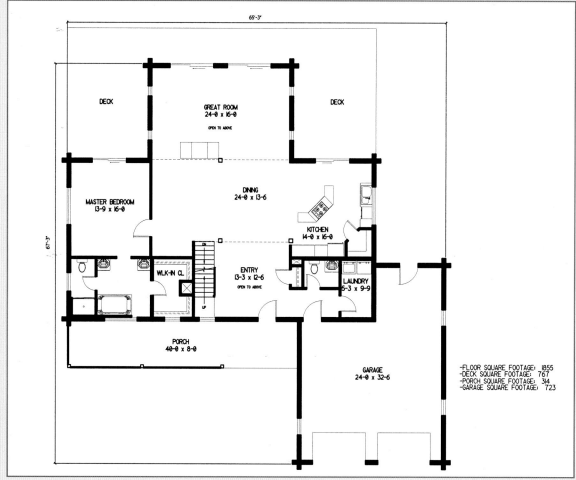

FIRST FLOOR PLAN

DECK

GREAT ROOM
24-0 x 16-0
OPEN TO ABOVE

DECK

MASTER BEDROOM
13-9 x 16-0

DINING
24-0 x 13-6

KITCHEN
14-0 x 16-0

WLK-IN CL

ENTRY
13-3 x 12-6
OPEN TO ABOVE

LAURY
5-3 x 9-9

PORCH
40-0 x 8-0

GARAGE
24-0 x 32-6

-FLOOR SQUARE FOOTAGE: 1855
-DECK SQUARE FOOTAGE: 767
-PORCH SQUARE FOOTAGE: 314
-GARAGE SQUARE FOOTAGE: 723

65'-3"

67'-3"

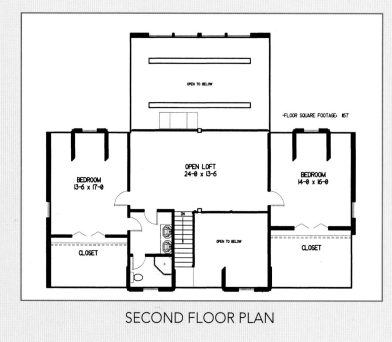

SECOND FLOOR PLAN

OPEN TO BELOW

-FLOOR SQUARE FOOTAGE: 1157

BEDROOM
13-6 x 17-0

OPEN LOFT
24-0 x 13-6

BEDROOM
14-0 x 16-0

CLOSET

OPEN TO BELOW

CLOSET

The large living room features a central fireplace and cathedral ceiling.

The two-sided fireplace also opens into the dining room of the "Seven Gables."

Cumberland Mountain

Hallmarks of the Gastineau Log Homes "Cumberland Mountain" include porches and decks.

Plan Title: **Cumberland Mountain**

Home Size: **2,786 square feet**

Plan Designer: **Gastineau Log Homes**

For more information, contact
Gastineau Log Homes, New Bloomfield, Missouri;
phone: 800-654-9253;
website: www.oakloghome.com.

Porches and decks are the hallmarks of this plan. Two wings off the central great room offer twin master suites, each with a private covered porch, cathedral ceiling, whirlpool tub, custom shower and double vanity.

The huge living room features exposed beam trusses in the cathedral ceiling, a fireplace and a solid gable of glass. The central staircase to the open loft provides privacy for the kitchen, which shares a beamed ceiling with the roomy dining area. The loft benefits from the large windows topping the great room, making it inviting bonus space.

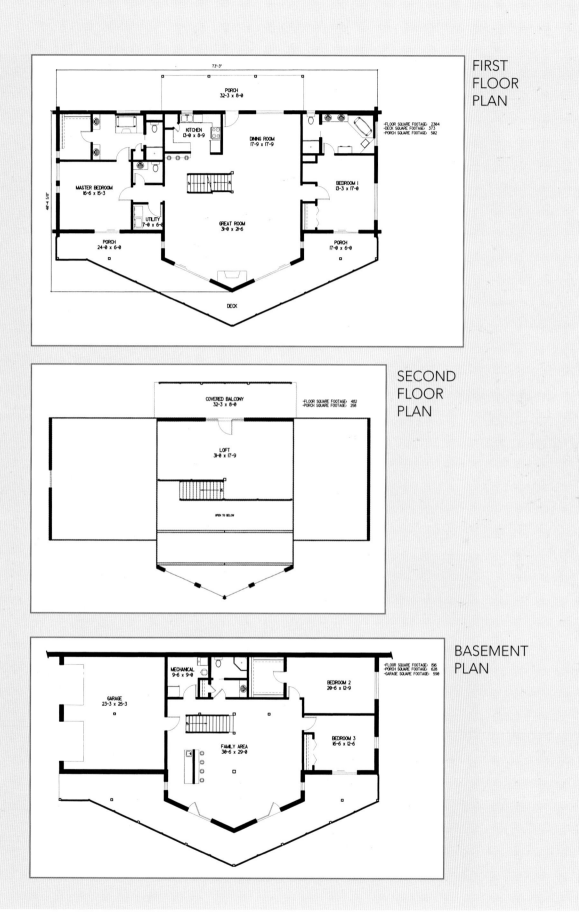

FIRST
FLOOR
PLAN

SECOND
FLOOR
PLAN

BASEMENT
PLAN

Plans From 2,000 to 4,000 Square Feet · **111**

Cumberland Mountain

The Cumberland Mountain's huge living room features exposed beam trusses in the cathedral ceiling, a fireplace and a solid gable of glass.

The private kitchen shares a beamed ceiling with the roomy dining room.

Two wings off the central great room offer twin master suites, each with a private covered porch.

Whirlpool tubs, custom showers and double vanities highlight the bathrooms of the twin master suites.

Double Eagle CV#1

Through the front door of the "Double Eagle CV#1" is a two-story foyer and a rambling great room.

Plan Title: **Double Eagle CV#1**

Home Size: **2,770 square feet**

Plan Designer: **Golden Eagle Log Homes**

For more information, contact
Golden Eagle Log Homes,
Wisconsin Rapids, Wisconsin; phone: 800-270-5025;
website: www.goldeneagleloghomes.com.

The two-story foyer signals this plan's openness, which is confirmed by the rambling great room, spanned by hand-peeled log tie beams. The open great room accesses a spacious rear deck.

The connection between the main level and the angled garage creates generous bonus space, which enlarges the kitchen work area and can accommodate a roomy pantry and laundry/mudroom.

The master bath is big enough for a separate shower and tub. The two loft bedrooms have their own baths and plenty of headroom, thanks to twin dormers.

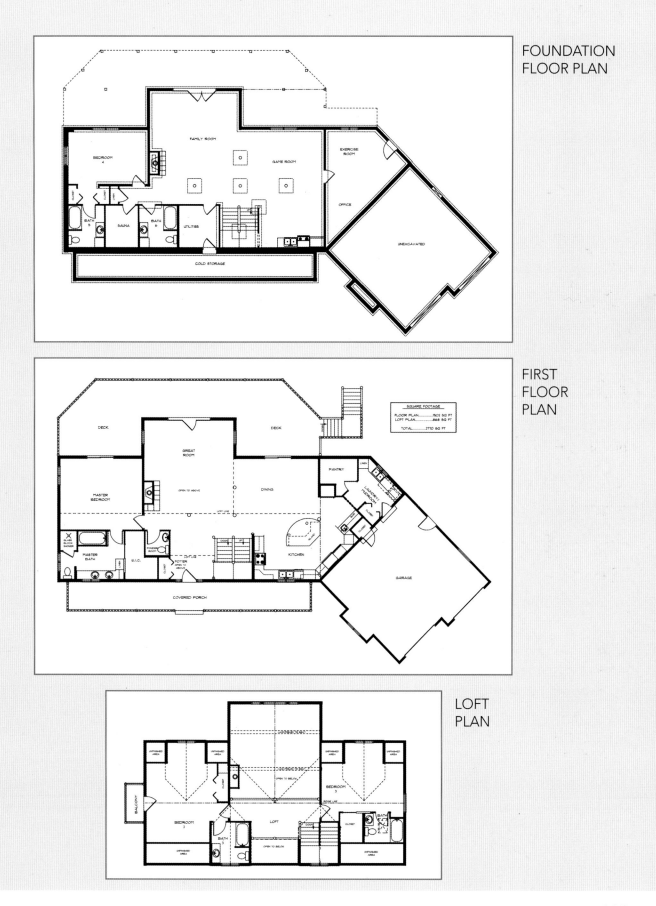

FOUNDATION
FLOOR PLAN

FIRST
FLOOR
PLAN

LOFT
PLAN

Custom #1

The rear deck of the Golden Eagle Log Homes "Custom #1" links the twin screen porches that access the master suite and dining room.

Plan Title: **Custom #1**

Home Size: **2,396 square feet**

Plan Designer: **Golden Eagle Log Homes**

For more information, contact
Golden Eagle Log Homes,
Wisconsin Rapids, Wisconsin; phone: 800-270-5025;
website: www.goldeneagleloghomes.com.

Distinctive quarter-round windows and a braced king-post truss punctuate the entry to this home. Twin screen porches, accessed from the master suite and dining room and linked by the rear deck, provide generous bonus space.

A beamed kitchen and dining area flows into the tall great room, which looks out at the deck and beyond through large windows and glass doors. Front and back dormers ensure headroom in the two loft bedrooms, each with its own bath.

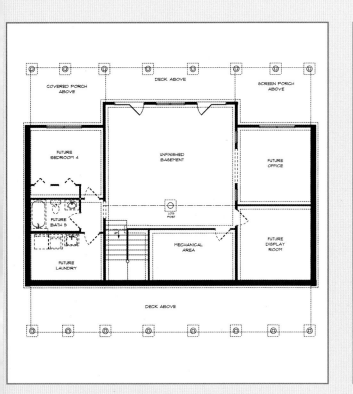

FOUNDATION FLOOR PLAN

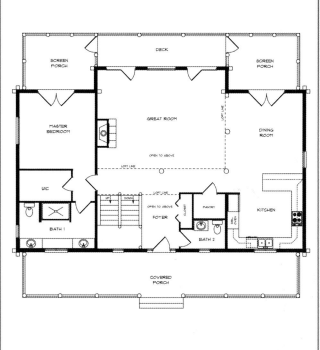

FIRST FLOOR PLAN

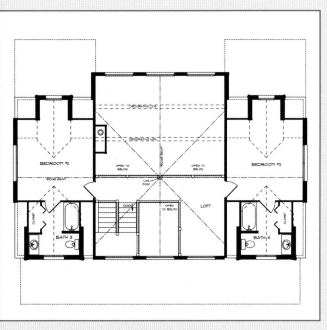

LOFT PLAN

A log staircase leading down to the basement and up to the loft is situated next to the foyer of the Golden Eagle Log Homes "Custom #1."

Custom #2

Walls of windows allow light into the great room, dining room and loft of the Golden Eagle Log Homes "Custom #2."

The side porch features accesses into the dining room and master bedroom.

Plan Title: **Custom #2**

Home Size: **2,010 square feet**

Plan Designer: **Golden Eagle Log Homes**

For more information, contact
Golden Eagle Log Homes,
Wisconsin Rapids, Wisconsin; phone: 800-270-5025;
website: www.goldeneagleloghomes.com.

The living area of the Golden Eagle Log Homes "Custom #2" is modest, saving room on the main level for the master suite, which spreads out beneath a beamed ceiling. The great room and dining area share a wall of windows, through which light can visually enlarge the space.

A small entry porch shelters access to the garage, while a side porch can be reached from the dining area and the master bedroom. The simple second-floor layout accommodates two bedrooms and a generous loft area serving a variety of uses.

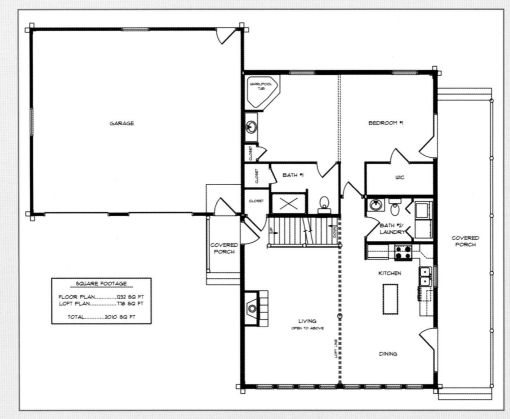

SQUARE FOOTAGE

FLOOR PLAN.............1232 SQ FT
LOFT PLAN................718 SQ FT

TOTAL.............2010 SQ FT

MAIN FLOOR PLAN

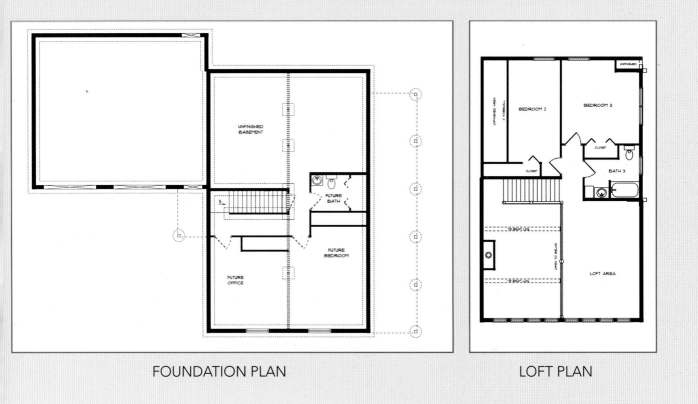

FOUNDATION PLAN

LOFT PLAN

Cottage Escape

Walls of windows, in the front and back of the Golden Eagle Log Homes "Cottage Escape," face out from either side of the great room. Accesses to the two decks in the back of the home are from the master suite and an entrance that leads to the great room.

Plan Title: **Cottage Escape**

Home Size: **3,268 square feet**

Plan Designer: **Golden Eagle Log Homes**

For more information, contact
Golden Eagle Log Homes,
Wisconsin Rapids, Wisconsin; phone: 800-270-5025;
website: www.goldeneagleloghomes.com.

Roominess and light characterize the "Cottage Escape" layout from Golden Eagle Log Homes. The open concept extends from the front of the home to the back of the house, including a dining room, kitchen and great room, with the kitchen taking a commanding stance.

The space connecting the garage allows for a sizable laundry room, a half bath and access to one of the decks. The master suite has a roomy bath and access to a second deck. Above is a second bedroom, well equipped to serve as the master bedroom or a guest suite, with a spacious loft overlooking the great room and sharing light from its windows.

MAIN FLOOR PLAN

LOFT PLAN

FOUNDATION PLAN

Chesapeake

Porches, decks and dormers are home features that complement the well-windowed great room of the "Chesapeake."

The three front dormers of the Kuhns Bros. Log Homes "Chesapeake" assure an interesting roofline, as well as plenty of interior room and light.

Plan Title: **Chesapeake**

Home Size: **2,769 square feet**

Plan Designer: **Kuhns Bros. Log Homes**

For more information, contact
Kuhns Bros. Log Homes, Lewisburg, Pennsylvania;
phone: 800-326-9614; website: www.kuhnsbros.com.

Porches, decks and plenty of storage highlight the Kuhns Bros. Log Homes "Chesapeake." The log home wraps around a central staircase and fireplace, which, in turn, lead in sequence to the great room, a dining room, the kitchen and entry, and the master suite. The spacious master suite features its own cathedral ceiling.

Three front dormers and two rear dormers echo the well-windowed great room and assure an interesting roofline, as well as plenty of interior room and light. Two upstairs bedrooms share a bath.

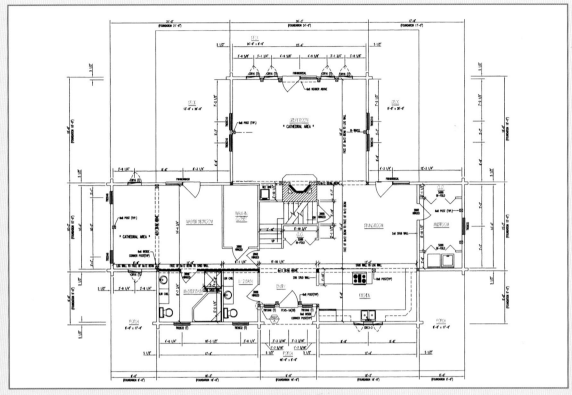

FIRST FLOOR PLAN

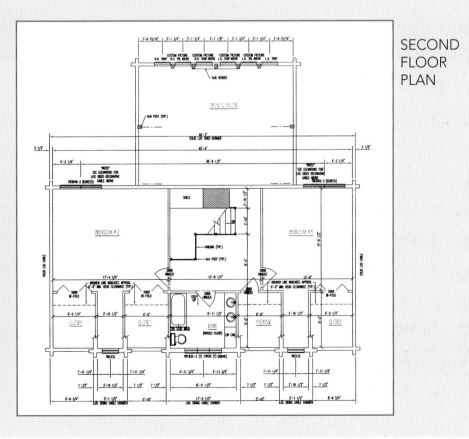

SECOND
FLOOR
PLAN

Keystone

The turret roofline and wall of windows highlight the exterior of the Kuhns Bros. Log Homes "Keystone."

Plan Title: Keystone

Home Size: 2,164 square feet

Plan Designer: Kuhns Bros. Log Homes

For more information, contact
Kuhns Bros. Log Homes, Lewisburg, Pennsylvania;
phone: 800-326-9614; website: www.kuhnsbros.com.

An octagonal sunroom with a turret roofline and a wall of windows highlight the exterior of the "Keystone." Inside, the main living area occupies more than half of the first level and features a cathedral ceiling atop the dining area, which leads to the sunroom.

Two bedrooms fill out the first floor. Upstairs, a small loft above the kitchen adjoins a roomy master suite. A shade porch spans the front of the home and wraps around to a deck off the dining and living area.

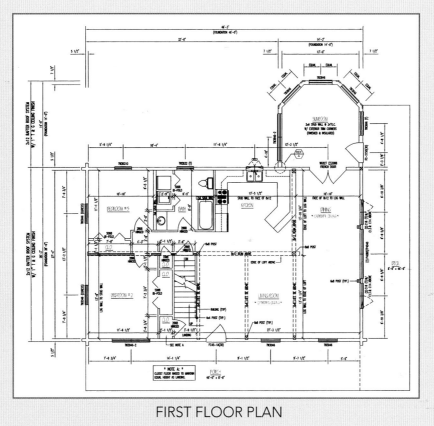

FIRST FLOOR PLAN

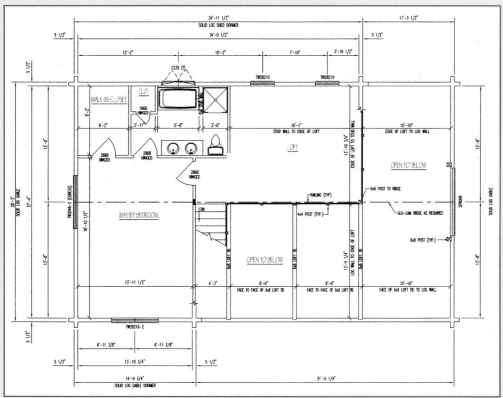

SECOND FLOOR PLAN

The Retreat

Packing extra space where it can, the two-story Hearthstone "The Retreat" includes a porch that is accessible from the kitchen.

Plan Title: **The Retreat**

Home Size: **2,800 square feet**

Plan Designer: **Hearthstone**

For more information, contact
Hearthstone, Dandridge, Tennessee;
phone: 800-247-4442;
website: www.hearthstonehomes.com.

The two-story plan packs extra space in where it can, including a sunroom, breakfast nook and office on the main level, as well as a porch that is accessible from the kitchen.

The compact master suite, entered to the left of the front door at the base of the stairs, enjoys privacy, while the office shares the living area's fireplace. The 30-by-40-foot second story contains two bedrooms, which share a bath, and a room-sized loft overlooking the living area.

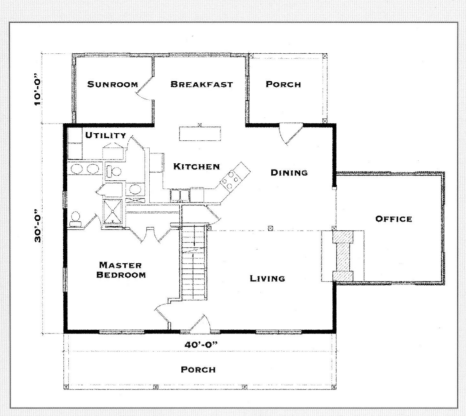

MAIN FLOOR PLAN

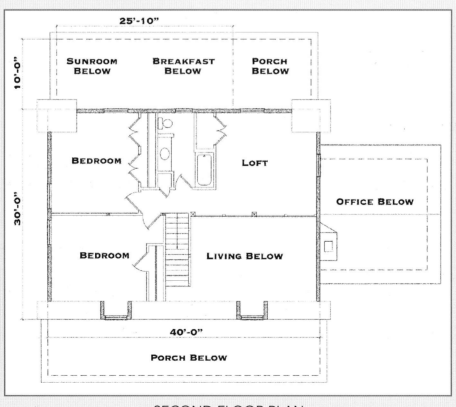

SECOND FLOOR PLAN

The Cannonsville

Plenty of window glass allows "The Cannonsville" from Beaver Mountain Log & Cedar Homes to take advantage of worthy views.

The generous great room opens to a broad deck that can also be accessed from the master suite.

Plan Title: **The Cannonsville**

Home Size: **3,676 square feet**

Plan Designer: **Beaver Mountain Log & Cedar Homes**

For more information, contact
Beaver Mountain Log & Cedar Homes,
Hancock, New York;
phone: 800-233-2770;
website: www.beavermtn.com.

Angled walls and abundant window glass allow this plan to take advantage of worthy views, while the generous great room opens to a broad deck. The deck can also be accessed from the master suite.

The master bath is as large as the kitchen, and a family room next to the kitchen adds to the informality of this layout. A spacious mudroom off the main entry connects to the two-car garage.

The upstairs allows versatility, with two bedrooms and baths, a sitting loft and a bonus room with windows on three sides that is big enough for a children's bunkroom or a substantial home office.

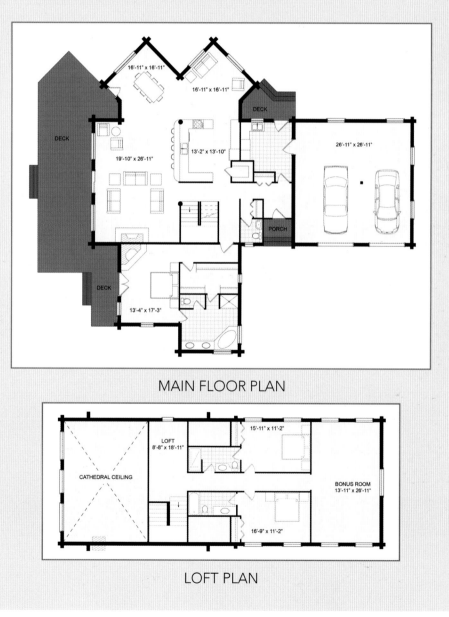

MAIN FLOOR PLAN

LOFT PLAN

The Mount Vernon

The decks and porch that surround "The Mount Vernon" from Beaver Mountain Log & Cedar Homes, as well as the dormers, help gain more space than indicated by the home's square footage.

The great room, master bedroom and mudroom open onto the back deck of "The Mount Vernon."

Plan Title: **The Mount Vernon**

Home Size: **3,006 square feet**

Plan Designer: **Beaver Mountain Log & Cedar Homes**

For more information, contact
Beaver Mountain Log & Cedar Homes,
Hancock, New York;
phone: 800-233-2770;
website: www.beavermtn.com.

This comfortably arranged layout gains even more space with decks and a porch that surround it. A formal entry opens through to the great room and leads to a convenient office adjacent to the luxurious master suite.

The large kitchen with bump-out breakfast nook opens to the living room and is partitioned from the formal dining room. The second floor has twin bedrooms, separated by a large loft, which also has a full bath.

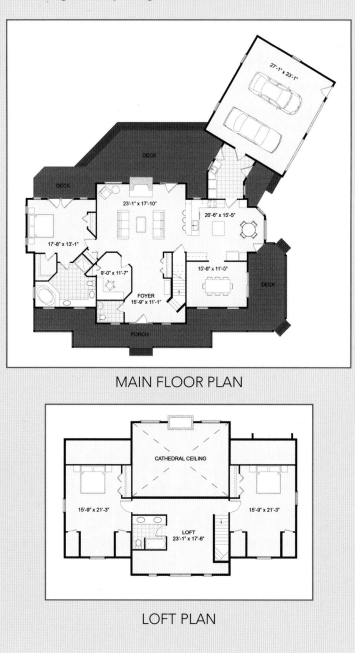

MAIN FLOOR PLAN

LOFT PLAN

The Saratoga Springs

The contemporary "shotgun" layout of "The Saratoga Springs" model from Beaver Mountain Log & Cedar Homes starts at the long foyer and leads past the kitchen and dining room to a generous living room.

Two decks extend off the rear of the home, including one off the oversized master suite and a second to the side of the great room and behind the mudroom and garage.

Plan Title: **The Saratoga Springs**

Home Size: **3,550 square feet**

Plan Designer: **Beaver Mountain Log & Cedar Homes**

For more information, contact
Beaver Mountain Log & Cedar Homes,
Hancock, New York;
phone: 800-233-2770;
website: www.beavermtn.com.

This contemporary "shotgun" layout starts at the long foyer and leads past the kitchen and dining room, beyond the central fireplace to a generous living room. A large mudroom links the kitchen and garage.

The highpoint of the main level is the oversized master suite with private deck. The real roominess is upstairs, which comprises a junior master suite with its own balcony, loft, two bedrooms above the garage, a full bath and an office.

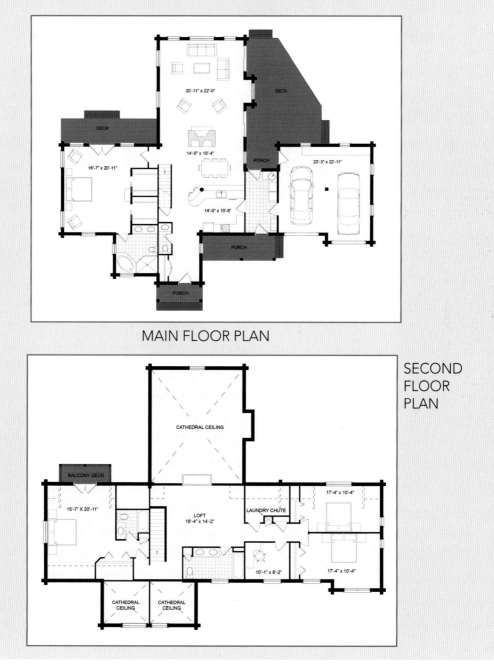

MAIN FLOOR PLAN

SECOND FLOOR PLAN

The Mountain View Retreat

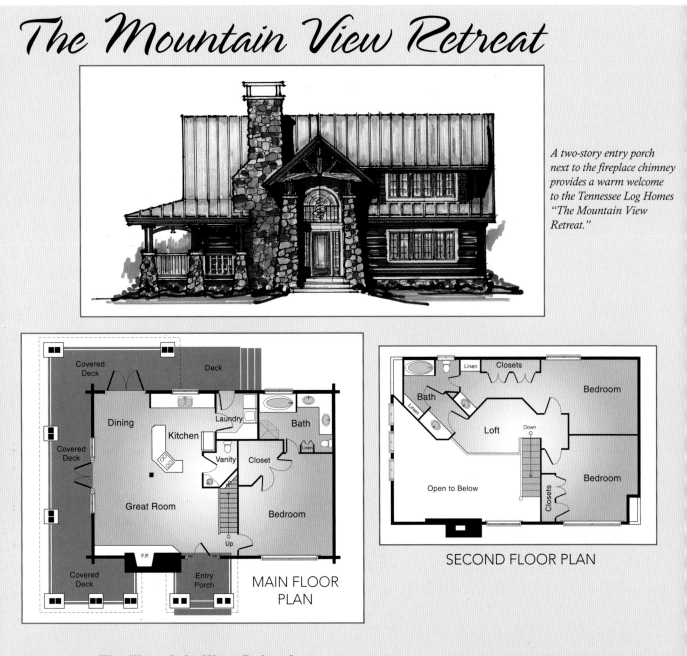

A two-story entry porch next to the fireplace chimney provides a warm welcome to the Tennessee Log Homes "The Mountain View Retreat."

MAIN FLOOR PLAN

Covered Deck · Deck · Dining · Laundry · Bath · Kitchen · Covered Deck · Vanity · Closet · Linen · Great Room · Bedroom · F.P. · Up · Covered Deck · Entry Porch

SECOND FLOOR PLAN

Linen · Closets · Bath · Bedroom · Linen · Loft · Down · Open to Below · Closets · Bedroom

Plan Title: **The Mountain View Retreat**

Home Size: **2,075 square feet**

Plan Designer: **Tennessee Log Homes**

For more information, contact Tennessee Log Homes, Athens, Tennessee; phone: 800-251-9218; website: www.tnloghomes.com.

A two-story entry porch next to the fireplace chimney provides a warm welcome to the Tennessee Log Homes "The Mountain View Retreat," while the wrap-around side porch accommodates a covered deck and covered outdoor dining area.

The main level comprises a master suite with a corner walk-in closet, a laundry room with outside entrance, and a large vaulted living room, dining area and kitchen. The loft above forms the kitchen's beamed ceiling. The second level has a "Jack-and-Jill" bathroom and identical twin bedrooms. The open loft is ideal as a sitting area or a media space.

The deck of "The Portland" connects to an ample great room with cathedral ceiling and double French doors.

Plan Title: **The Portland**

Home Size: **2,046 square feet**

Plan Designer:

Original Old Timer Log Homes & Supply

For more information, contact
Original Old Timer Log Homes & Supply,
Mount Juliet, Tennessee; phone: 800-467-3006;
website: www.oldtimerloghomes.com.

A large, covered porch and broad deck provide extra living space to "The Portland" from Original Old Timer Log Homes & Supply. The deck connects to an ample great room with cathedral ceiling and double French doors. The kitchen features a beamed ceiling, and a stone-and-wood eat-at island opens to the dining area and living room.

Located on the main level are a full bath, laundry room and two bedrooms, each with a walk-in closet. The master suite, located upstairs, features a large walk-in closet, private bath and a loft that is ideal for a sitting area or a small home office.

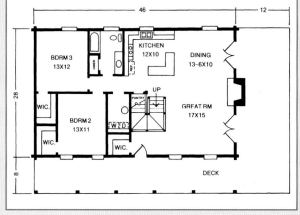

MAIN FLOOR PLAN

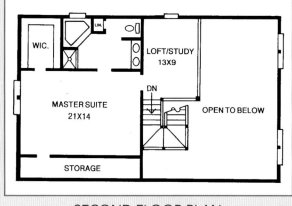

SECOND FLOOR PLAN

The Portland

The kitchen opens to the dining area and living room.

The cathedral ceiling of the great room opens up the concept of "The Portland" and gives it an airy, non-cramped feel.

The kitchen features a beamed ceiling, and a stone-and-wood eat-at island.

The loft of the Original Old Timer Log Homes & Supply "The Portland" is ideal for a sitting area or a small home office.

Located upstairs, the master suite showcases a large walk-in closet and a private bath.

The Breckenridge

Both wings of the Yellowstone Log Homes "Breckenridge" access the wide, 52-foot deck. A covered entry leads to the foyer that, in turn, opens to a living room punctuated by a towering wall of windows.

Plan Title: **The Breckenridge**

Home Size: **2,410 square feet**

Plan Designer: **Yellowstone Log Homes**

For more, contact
Yellowstone Log Homes, Rigby, Idaho;
phone: 208-745-8108;
website: www.yellowstoneloghomes.com.

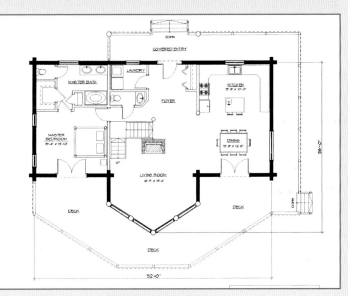

MAIN FLOOR PLAN

A covered entry leads to a foyer that, in turn, opens to a living room punctuated by a towering wall of windows. The symmetrical layout includes a kitchen and dining area on one side of the living room and a master suite to the other. Both wings access the wide, 52-foot deck. Upstairs, a central loft divides two bedrooms that share a bath but have their own balconies.

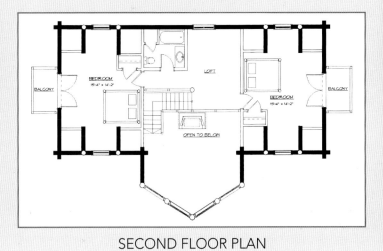

SECOND FLOOR PLAN

The Columbia

The wrap-around main porch of "The Columbia" from Original Old Timer Log Homes & Supply adds living space outdoors and accesses from the front door, living room, dining area, kitchen and utility room.

Plan Title: **The Columbia**

Home Size: **2,915 square feet**

Plan Designer: **Original Old Timer Log Homes & Supply**

For more information, contact Original Old Timer Log Homes & Supply, Mount Juliet, Tennessee; phone: 800-467-3006; website: www.oldtimerloghomes.com.

This layout allows for a spacious, open living area with stone fireplace, soaring cathedral ceiling and custom beam trusses. The large kitchen is designed to take full advantage of the dining area and great room. The master bedroom, located on the main floor, features a luxurious bath, a walk-in closet and French doors that lead to its own porch.

Two bedrooms, a full bath and a storage space are located upstairs. The balcony area could serve as a cozy sitting or reading space. The wrap-around main porch adds living room with accesses from the front door, living room, dining area, kitchen and utility room.

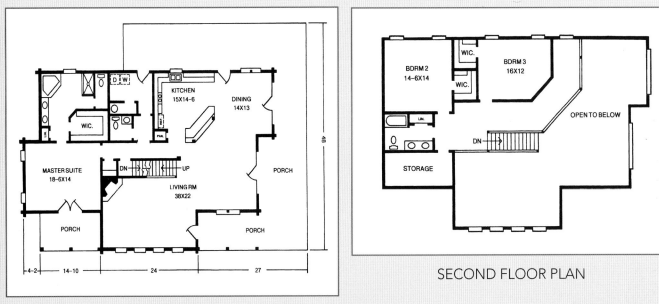

MAIN FLOOR PLAN

SECOND FLOOR PLAN

The large kitchen of "The Columbia" is designed to take full advantage of the dining area and great room.

A cathedral ceiling and custom beam trusses soar over the open living area with stone fireplace.

The master bedroom, located on the main floor, features a luxurious bath.

Riverbend

Plan Title: Riverbend

Home Size: 2,453 square feet

Plan Designer: Strongwood Log Home Company

For more, contact
Strongwood Log Home Co.,
Waupaca, Wisconsin; phone: 866-258-4818;
website: www.strongwoodloghomes.com.

Distinguished by a prow front, floor-to-ceiling windows and soaring rooflines, this design is particularly suited for property with views in several directions. What's more, the prow angle can be modified to capture specific views.

Balancing the windows in the central great room is a two-sided fireplace with built-in bench. The master bedroom and a second bedroom, each with its own bath, occupy one wing. Above, a catwalk spanning the great room links a loft and a third bedroom, also with its own bath.

The master bedroom and a second bedroom, each with its own bath, occupy one wing of the Strongwood Log Home Company "Riverbend".

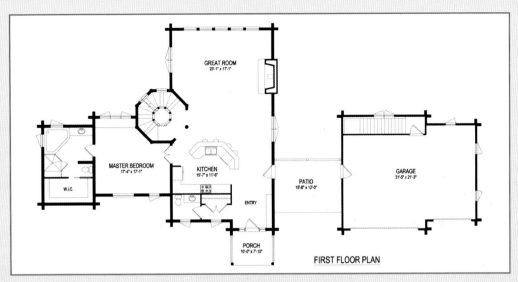

FIRST FLOOR PLAN

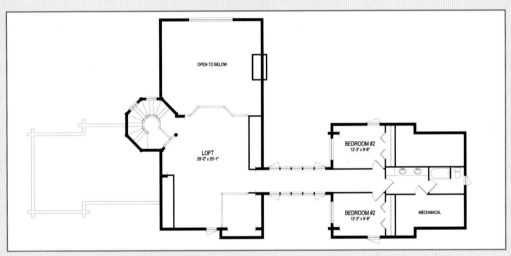

SECOND FLOOR PLAN

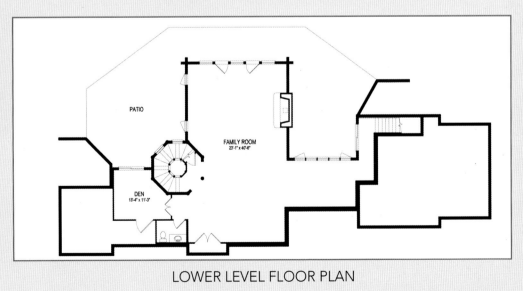

LOWER LEVEL FLOOR PLAN

Clearwater

Nearly every room of the Strongwood Log Home Company "Clearwater" enjoys a view. The large, screened porch, decks and a lower-level terrace provide ample space for three-season outdoor living.

Plan Title: **Clearwater**

Home Size: **3,318 square feet**

Plan Designer: **Strongwood Log Home Company**

For more, contact
Strongwood Log Home Co.,
Waupaca, Wisconsin; phone: 866-258-4818;
website: www.strongwoodloghomes.com.

Designed originally as a waterfront retreat, this compact plan is arranged so nearly every room enjoys a view. The main living area occupies 2,228 square feet on the first and loft levels, while a finished lower level serves as a guest suite, comprising living and kitchen areas and two bedrooms.

The large screened porch, decks and a lower-level terrace provide ample space for three-season outdoor living. The master bedroom has its own deck, and two upstairs bedrooms parade private balconies.

FIRST FLOOR PLAN

SECOND FLOOR PLAN

LOWER LEVEL FLOOR PLAN

A loft / hallway connects the two upstairs bedrooms, and each accesses its own balcony.

Nantucket

The Strongwood Log Home Company "Nantucket" is defined by an efficient layout, including large windows that flank the chimney, a roomy deck in the back of the home that serves the master bedroom and dining area, and an attached garage featuring two bays.

Plan Title: **Nantucket**

Home Size: **2,012 square feet**

Plan Designer: **Strongwood Log Home Company**

For more, contact
Strongwood Log Home Co.,
Waupaca, Wisconsin; phone: 866-258-4818;
website: www.strongwoodloghomes.com.

A simple but efficient layout groups the living room, dining area and kitchen next to a powder room and laundry room that help partition this section from the master suite. The living room windows flank the fireplace, which extends to the open ceiling above.

Stairs lead to a small loft and two upstairs bedrooms, which share a bathroom. A roomy deck serves the master bedroom and dining area. The attached garage features two bays.

MASTER BEDROOM
14'-0" x 16'-0"

KITCHEN
14'-3" x 9'-0"

DINING ROOM
11'-6" x 9'-0"

LIVING ROOM
22'-2" x 13'-7"

PORCH
24'-0" x 6'-0"

GARAGE
28'-0" x 28'-0"

FIRST FLOOR PLAN

FIRST FLOOR PLAN

BEDROOM #2
13'-0" x 11'-0"

LOFT
11'-5" x 12'-7"

BEDROOM #3
13'-0" x 10'-5"

OPEN TO BELOW

SECOND FLOOR PLAN

SECOND FLOOR PLAN

The Nantucket kitchen, with exposed ceiling beams, exhibits plenty of counter and cabinet space.

The living room, dining area and kitchen of the "Nantucket" are grouped in an efficient layout, with the living room having a high, open ceiling above.

Yorke

Sprawling decks, a front entryway with long overhang, large windows, exposed logs and multiple rooflines combine to define the "Yorke" from Real Log Homes.

Plan Title: Yorke

Home Size: 3,945 square feet

Plan Designer: Real Log Homes

For more, contact
Real Log Homes, Hartland, Vermont;
phone: 800-732-5564;
website: www.realloghomes.com.

The kitchen and dining room, and second-floor bedrooms open to the living and foyer areas, which are capped by a cathedral ceiling, all creating a family-friendly focal point. The living area features a two-sided fireplace and a three-story spiral staircase.

One bedroom is on the main level, but the master suite is tucked away on the upper level. A catwalk overlooking the long living area links to two smaller bedrooms on either side of the stairs. The master bedroom has its own balcony, above the deck, which can be accessed through two sets of double doors.

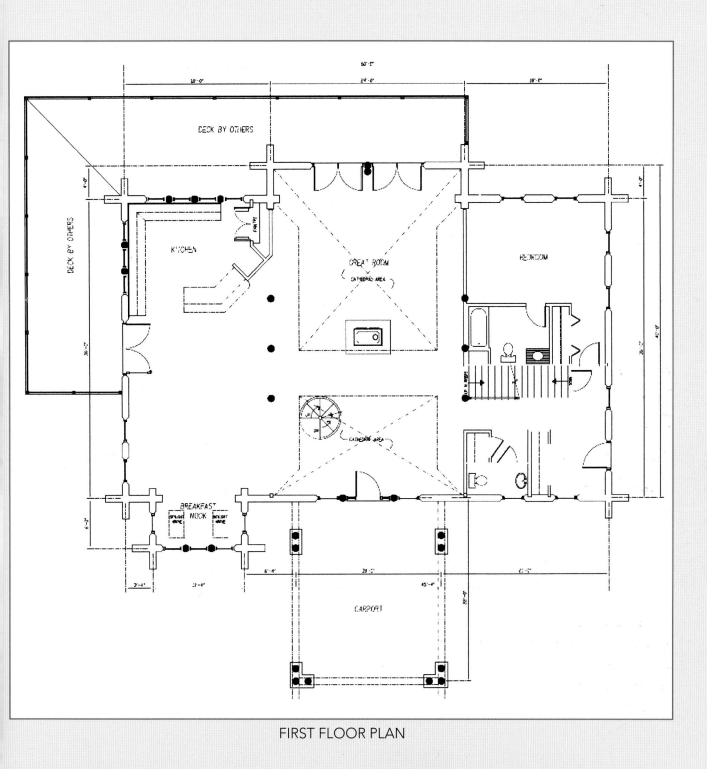

FIRST FLOOR PLAN

Yorke

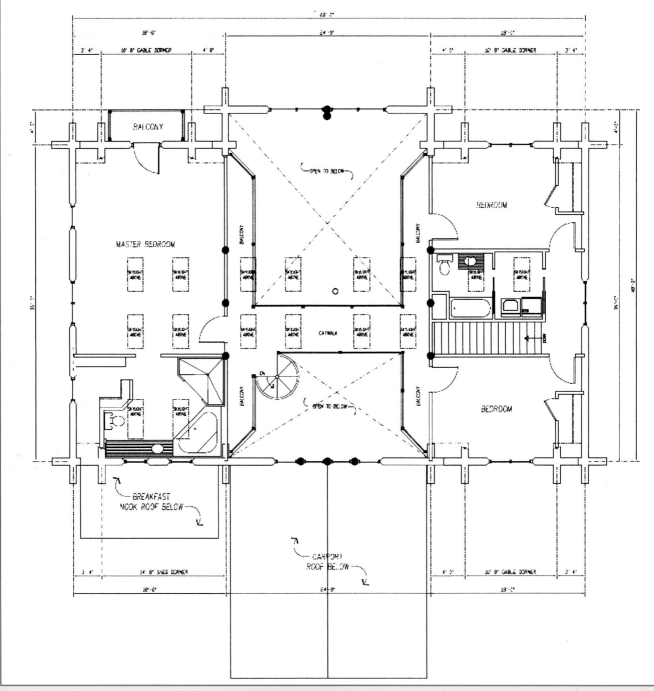

SECOND FLOOR PLAN

The kitchen and dining room of the "Yorke" open to the living and foyer area.

The living and foyer areas of the "Yorke" are capped by a cathedral ceiling and create a family-friendly focal point.

The living area features a three-story spiral staircase.

Plans From 2,000 to 4,000 Square Feet · **149**

Cutrell

The vaulted entry area of the Real Log Homes "Cutrell" opens into a grand cathedral-style room. A patio door off the back corner of the loft leads to a balcony.

Plan Title: **Cutrell**

Home Size: **3,550 square feet**

Plan Designer: **Real Log Homes**

For more, contact
Real Log Homes, Hartland, Vermont;
phone: 800-732-5564;
website: www.realloghomes.com.

The great room features exposed log roof rafters, patio doors and step-up windows.

The vaulted entry area opens into a grand cathedral-style great room featuring exposed log roof rafters, patio doors and step-up windows. The open living space is highlighted by an L-shaped kitchen, which adjoins a sunroom that opens to the deck.

The first-floor master bedroom showcases a walkout window bay. Stairs lead to a large second bedroom, which opens to a study and a loft above the dining area. A patio door off the back corner of the loft leads to a balcony. A breezeway connects to a 792-square-foot recreation room.

The open living space is highlighted by an L-shaped kitchen, which adjoins a sunroom that opens to the deck.

FIRST FLOOR PLAN

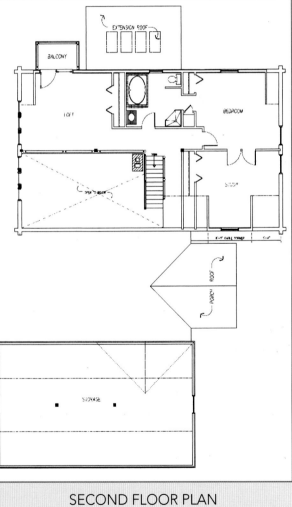

SECOND FLOOR PLAN

Conger / Dabbs

The Real Log Homes "Conger/
Dabbs" model is a two-bedroom,
two-and-a-half bath Cape Cod with a
full-length front porch and a screened
porch in back.

Plan Title: **Conger/Dabbs**

Home Size: **2,060 square feet**

Plan Designer: **Real Log Homes**

For more, contact
Real Log Homes, Hartland, Vermont;
phone: 800-732-5564;
website: www.realloghomes.com.

The first floor of this two-bedroom, two-and-a-half bath Cape features a compact kitchen, living room and semi-formal dining room, reserving nearly half the main-floor square footage for the master suite. Half of that space is devoted to the walk-in closet and roomy bathroom with a whirlpool tub and tiled shower.

The full-length front porch adds charm, while the screen porch adds functionality. The upper level consists of a bedroom and bath, ample storage space and a loft overlooking the great room.

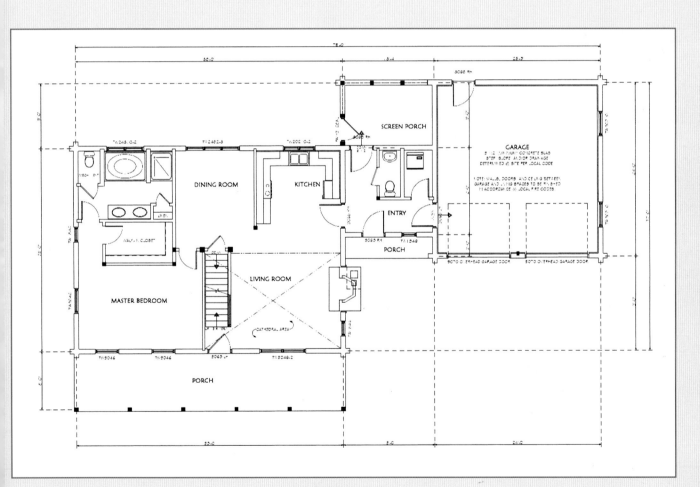

FIRST FLOOR PLAN

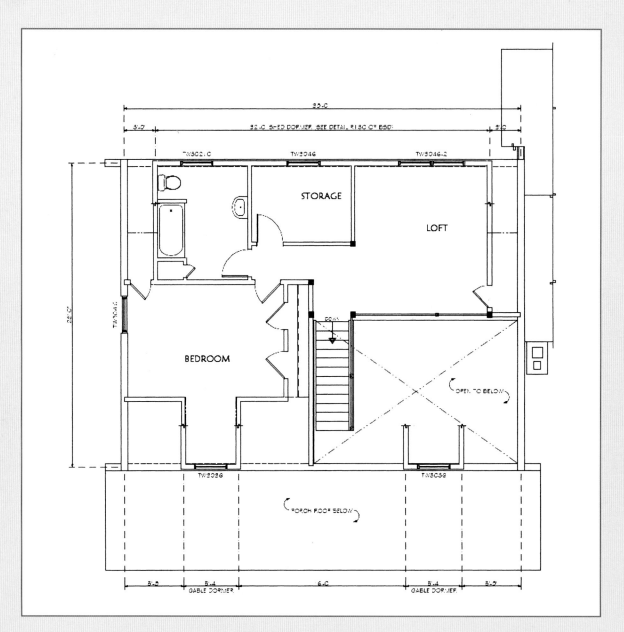

SECOND FLOOR PLAN

A loft overlooks the expansive great room of the Real Log Homes "Conger/Dabbs."

A wall separates the otherwise open and airy kitchen and semi-formal dining room.

Badger Peak

The outside living spaces of the Wisconsin Log Homes "Badger Peak" are harmonized using architectural elements like an octagonal gazebo, porches and expansive decking.

Plan Title: **Badger Peak**

Home Size: **3,389 square feet**

Plan Designer: **Wisconsin Log Homes**

For more, contact
Wisconsin Log Homes, Green Bay, Wisconsin;
phone: 800-844-7970;
website: www.wisconsinloghomes.com.

Soaring windows make the central great room perfect for showcasing surrounding views, while an artful staircase adds natural drama. The roomy main-floor master suite and laundry room anchor the single-floor living arrangement, while two bedrooms and a full bath upstairs are nestled behind the roomy loft. Outdoor living spaces are harmonized using architectural elements, like an octagon gazebo, porches and expansive decking.

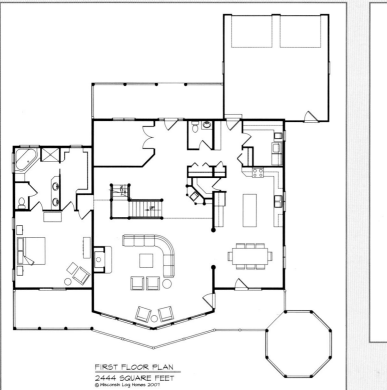

FIRST FLOOR PLAN
2444 SQUARE FEET
© Wisconsin Log Homes 2007

MAIN FLOOR PLAN

SECOND FLOOR PLAN
945 SQUARE FEET
© Wisconsin Log Homes 2007

SECOND FLOOR PLAN

An artful staircase adds natural drama.

Badger Peak

Soaring windows make the central great room of the "Badger Peak" perfect for showcasing surrounding views.

The open concept of the home, especially with the high ceilings and numerous glass doors and windows, give it an open, airy feel.

Lakeview

The wall of glass in the great room of the Katahdin Cedar Log Homes "Lakeview" provides an unimpeded view to nature surrounding the back of the home. Decks add to the home's appearance and living space.

Plan Title: Lakeview

Home Size: 2,360 square feet

Plan Designer: Katahdin Cedar Log Homes

For more, contact
Katahdin Cedar Log Homes,
Oakfield, Maine; phone: 800-845-4533;
website: www.katahdincedarloghomes.com.

This open-concept home boasts a cathedral ceiling over the entry and living rooms, and a spectacular wall of glass in the great room, providing an unimpeded view. Flanking the great room are the kitchen and dining area on one side, with their own deck, and the master suite, also with a deck, on the other.

The decks add to the home's appearance and living space. This home also features a distinctive inside balcony overlooking the great room and linking twin bedrooms.

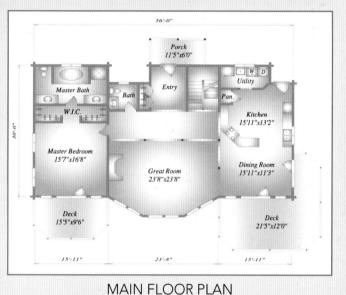

MAIN FLOOR PLAN

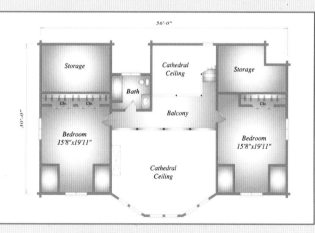

SECOND FLOOR PLAN

Bonanza

The Katahdin Cedar Log Homes "Bonanza" benefits from an extensive wrap-around porch and spacious front deck. Abundant windows adorn the front of the home, allowing plenty of light and views.

Plan Title: **Bonanza**

Home Size: **2,890 square feet**

Plan Designer: **Katahdin Cedar Log Homes**

For more, contact
Katahdin Cedar Log Homes,
Oakfield, Maine; phone: 800-845-4533;
website: www.katahdincedarloghomes.com.

A central great room connects to flanking bedroom wings. The smaller of the two wings features a bedroom with its own bathroom and is backed by a generous laundry room. The larger holds a spacious master suite, highlighted by the luxurious bathroom.

Upstairs, two additional bedrooms, each with its own bath and walk-in closet, share a loft that overlooks the great room. The home also benefits from an extensive wrap-around porch and spacious front deck. Abundant windows adorn the front of the home, allowing plenty of light and views.

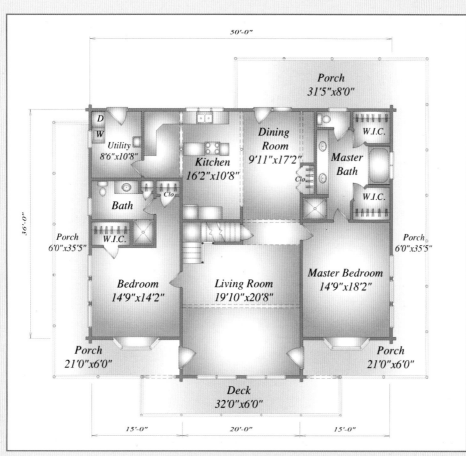

MAIN FLOOR PLAN

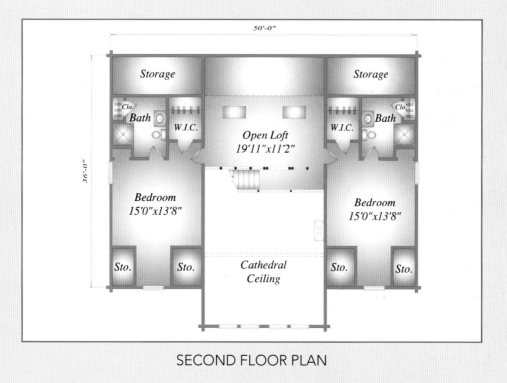

SECOND FLOOR PLAN

The Timber

A king-post truss distinguishes the built-up entry of "The Timber" from Yellowstone Log Homes, and the truss matches the pitch of the main roof and dormers.

Plan Title: The Timber

Home Size: 2,640 square feet

Plan Designer: Yellowstone Log Homes

For more, contact
Yellowstone Log Homes, Rigby, Idaho;
phone: 208-745-8108;
website: www.yellowstoneloghomes.com.

A king-post truss distinguishes the built-up entry, which matches the pitch of the main roof and dormers. The foyer transitions to the rectangular great room, which projects onto the deck. The dining area and L-shaped kitchen occupy one wing; the opposite wing is given over to the master suite.

Upstairs, front and rear dormers add light and headroom to twin bedrooms, separated by a bath and loft open to the great room. The rear dormers open to private balconies. An attached garage, accessible from the kitchen, adds 584 square feet to the plan.

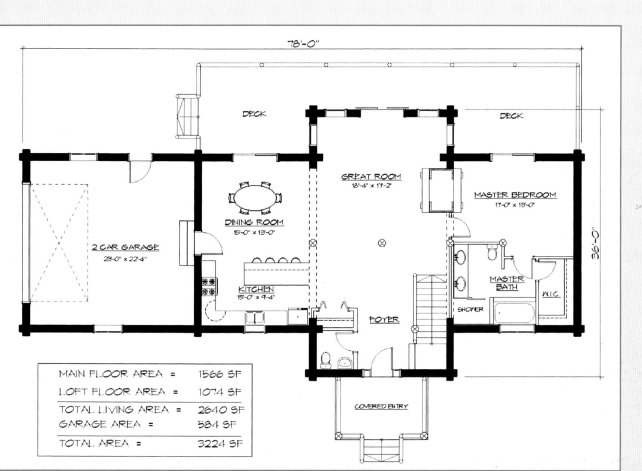

MAIN FLOOR PLAN

MAIN FLOOR AREA =	1566 SF
LOFT FLOOR AREA =	1074 SF
TOTAL LIVING AREA =	2640 SF
GARAGE AREA =	584 SF
TOTAL AREA =	3224 SF

78'-0"

36'-0"

DECK

DECK

GREAT ROOM
18'-4" x 17'-2"

MASTER BEDROOM
17'-0" x 13'-0"

DINING ROOM
15'-0" x 13'-0"

2 CAR GARAGE
29'-0" x 22'-4"

KITCHEN
15'-0" x 9'-4"

MASTER BATH

W.I.C.

SHOWER

FOYER

COVERED ENTRY

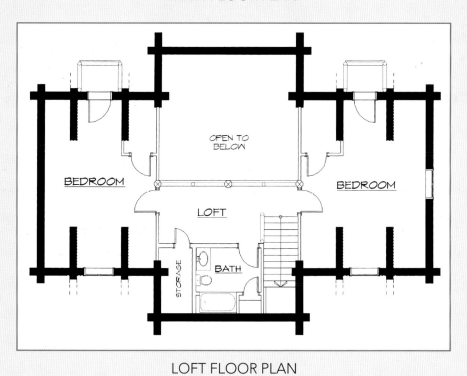

LOFT FLOOR PLAN

OPEN TO BELOW

BEDROOM

BEDROOM

LOFT

STORAGE

BATH

Elk River II

Plan Title: **Elk River II**

Home Size: **2,234 square feet**

Plan Designer: **StoneMill Log Homes**

For more, contact
StoneMill Log Homes, Knoxville, Tennessee;
phone: 800-438-8274;
website: www.stonemill.com.

The spacious great room dominates the layout and accesses the wide front deck and a smaller screened deck in the back. A tucked-away kitchen and dining area form one wing, which is balanced by the first-floor master suite. The master suite enjoys its own access to the porch.

Two upper-level bedrooms share a bathroom and small loft area overlooking the great room. A novel feature is the side porch, which is accessible from the dining area and adds outdoor space for informal dining.

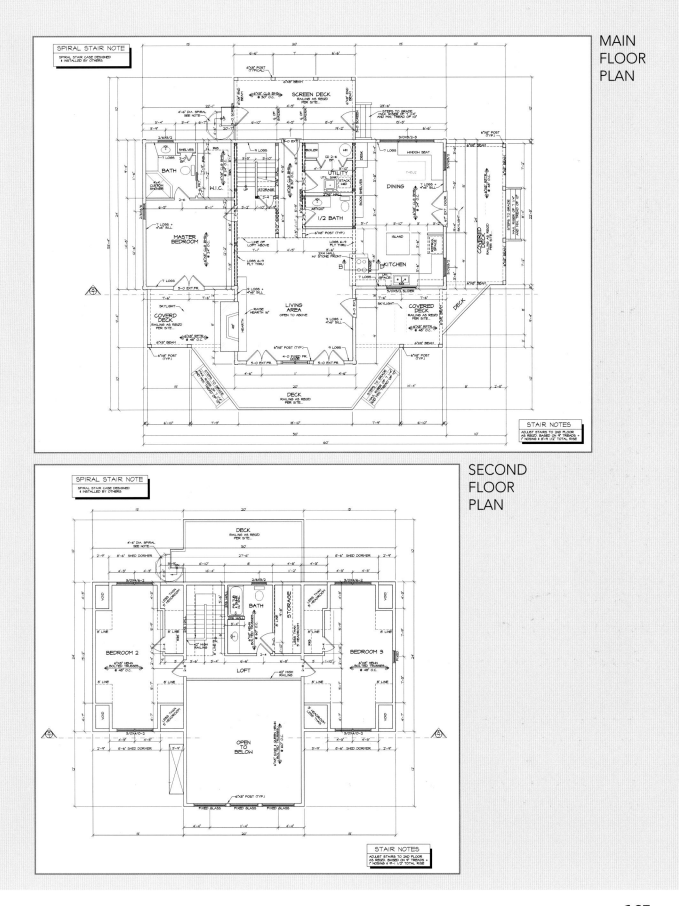

MAIN
FLOOR
PLAN

SECOND
FLOOR
PLAN

Elk River II

A spacious great room with massive windows dominates the "Elk River II" from StoneMill Log Homes.

A tucked-away kitchen and dining area form one wing of the "Elk River II," which is balanced by the first-floor master suite.

Kelley Plantation

Plan Title: **Kelley Plantation**

Home Size: **2,693 square feet**

Plan Designer: **StoneMill Log Homes**

For more, contact
StoneMill Log Homes, Knoxville, Tennessee;
phone: 800-438-8274;
website: www.stonemill.com.

The efficient and conveniently designed plan features a spacious master suite on the main level with a walk-in closet and master bath. The large great room is centrally located to all rooms, and the foyer transitions from the porch to the living and dining rooms.

Twin doors flanking the fireplace lead to the rear deck. A sunroom off the living room is also accessible from the master bath, making it the perfect relaxation spot. Two small bedrooms on the upper level share a bathroom.

Efficient and conveniently designed, the "Kelley Plantation" from StoneMill Log Homes transitions from a front porch to a foyer and then to the living and dining rooms.

Kelley Plantation

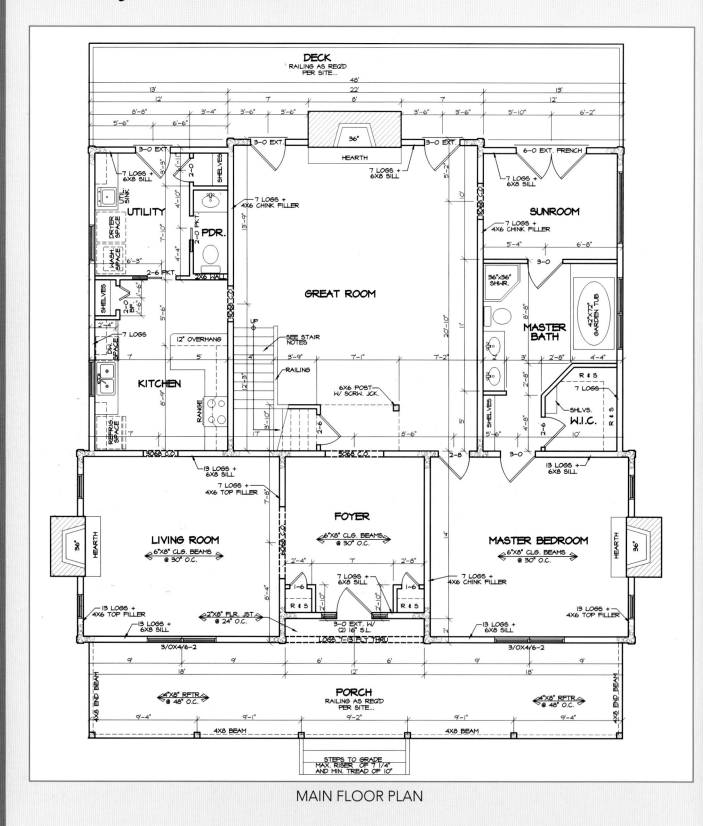

MAIN FLOOR PLAN

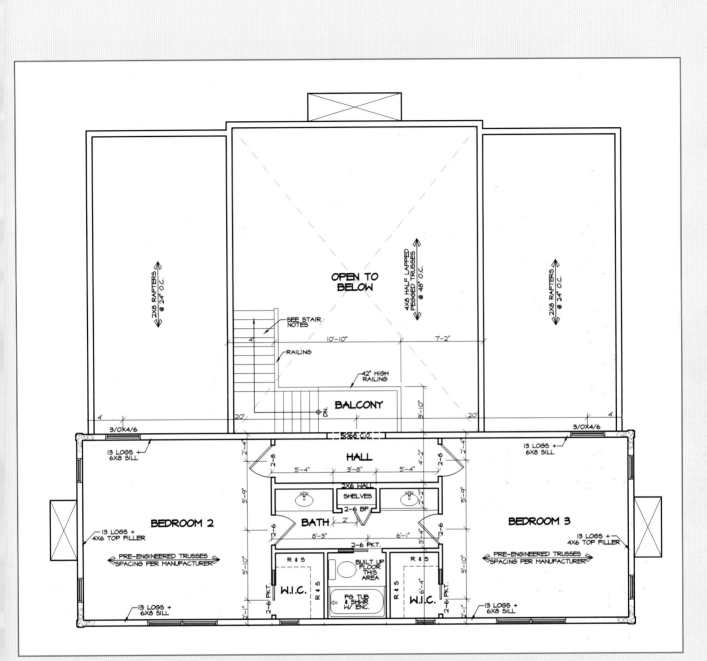

SECOND FLOOR PLAN

Kelley Plantation

The large great room is centrally located to all rooms.

The living and dining rooms of the "Kelley Plantation" are connected.

A spacious master suite on the main level of the "Kelley Plantation" features a walk-in closet and master bath.

The Caribou

One-level living maximizes the space of "The Caribou" from PrecisionCraft and Mountain Architects. Patios surround the home to extend the living space outdoors.

Plan Title: **The Caribou**

Home Size: **2,166 square feet**

Plan Designer: **PrecisionCraft and Mountain Architects**

For more, contact
PrecisionCraft Log & Timber
Homes, Meridian, Idaho;
phone: 800-729-1320;
website: www.precisioncraft.com.

One-level living maximizes the space available, providing three bedrooms, including the master suite, which shares a fireplace with the living room and opens to a patio that has its own outdoor fireplace. A cluster of bathrooms and the laundry room separate the master suite from the remaining bedrooms, which are located down a hall from the entry.

The great room bumps out to accommodate the dining room and kitchen. Patios surround the home to extend the living space outdoors.

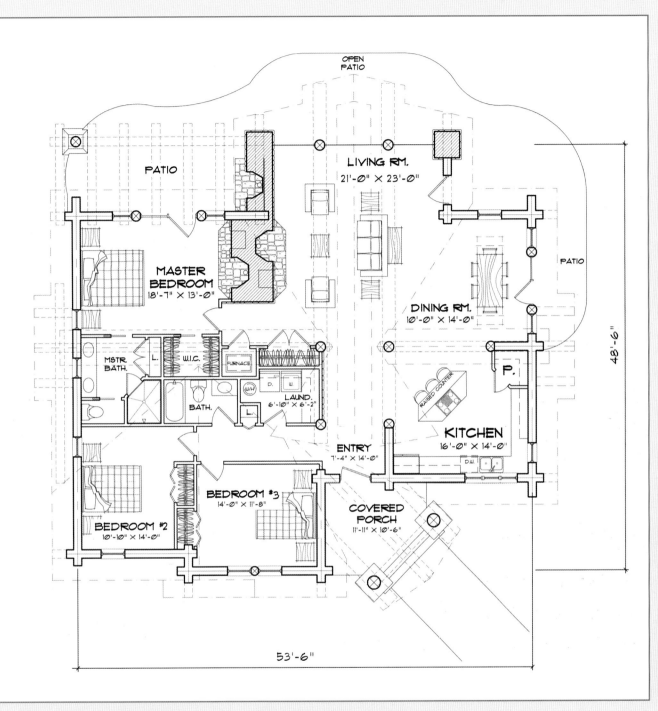

OPEN PATIO

PATIO

LIVING RM.
21'-0" × 23'-0"

MASTER BEDROOM
18'-7" × 13'-0"

PATIO

DINING RM.
10'-0" × 14'-0"

MSTR. BATH.

L.

W.I.C.

FURNACE

W/H

D.

W.

LAUND.
6'-10" × 6'-2"

L.

BATH.

P.

RAISED COUNTER

KITCHEN
16'-0" × 14'-0"

D.W.

ENTRY
7'-4" × 14'-0"

BEDROOM #3
14'-0" × 11'-8"

BEDROOM #2
10'-10" × 14'-0"

COVERED PORCH
11'-11" × 10'-6"

48'-6"

53'-6"

MAIN FLOOR PLAN

The McCall

The efficient layout of "The McCall" is perfect for taking in spectacular views.

Plan Title: **The McCall**

Home Size: **2,408 square feet**

Plan Designer: **Lodge Logs**

For more, contact
Lodge Logs, Boise, Idaho;
phone: 800-533-2450;
website: www.lodgelogs.com.

Perfect for taking in spectacular views, as well as entertaining family and friends, the efficient layout includes three bedrooms and an open great room.

The first floor showcases a large living room with access to a deck, a dining room/kitchen area, pantry and master suite, the latter of which includes a bath and walk-in closet. Upstairs are two bedrooms, a bath, loft area and plenty of storage space.

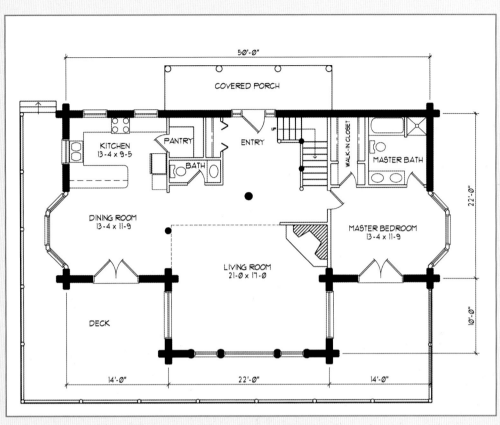

MAIN FLOOR PLAN

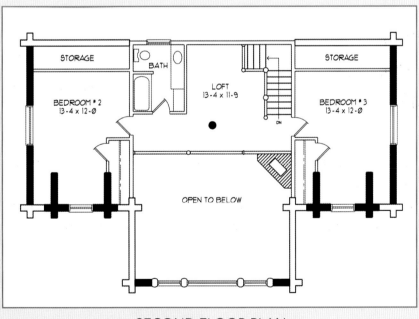

SECOND FLOOR PLAN

The McCall

The open great room is just one place in "The McCall" to enjoy those spectacular outdoor views.

The first floor showcases a dining room/kitchen area and pantry.

The Wyoming

Four decks and porches and a contemporary design elevate "The Wyoming" from Lodge Logs as one of the "100 Best Log Home Floor Plans."

Plan Title: **The Wyoming**

Home Size: **2,357 square feet**

Plan Designer: **Lodge Logs**

For more, contact
Lodge Logs, Boise, Idaho;
phone: 800-533-2450;
website: www.lodgelogs.com.

The Wyoming

With four bedrooms, covered decks and porches, and a contemporary design, this plan is for people who want a little more out of their cabin. From the covered entry, one enters a utility room next to the master suite, and then a unique dining room with six windowed sides. The dining room flows into an open kitchen and spacious great room.

The second floor awaits and includes three bedrooms, a bath and a loft that overlooks the great room.

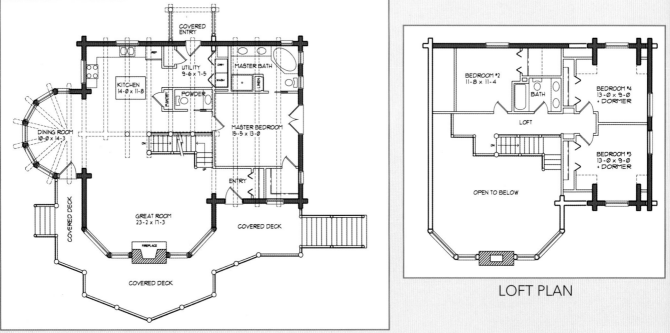

MAIN FLOOR PLAN

LOFT PLAN

The dining room flows into an open kitchen and spacious great room.

Big Plans Start With

The following parade of log homes includes those with more than 4,000 total square feet

For many log-home buyers, big is the only way to go. This is especially true if you are moving up from an existing place into what you envision as your ultimate dream home. A big house will offer ample extra space for rooms that might not fit into your present home: the family room, library, den, walk-in closets, guest suite, fitness and hobby rooms, and so on.

The trouble is that people who are "moving on up" often neglect to properly plan out the extra space. Adding square footage isn't enough. You need to use it to your best advantage.

Today's large homes incorporate expansive, open-concept living rooms and great rooms to allow more entertaining space, as well as to accommodate custom-designed furniture. The bedrooms of large homes have also evolved. Master bedroom suites with luxury baths are being incorporated into the floor plans, along with guest bedrooms that include their own baths for guest privacy.

There are some exterior trends in large homes, too. Lots of fixed glass is being used in angled or prow walls. Sometimes there is more glass than wood in certain walls of homes, as well as in the living room and great room areas.

Buyers are adding dormers to create roof character and better utilize the upper-story floor spaces in their designs. Bay windows and turrets are popular for the dining room/breakfast nook rooms, as well as in some baths with sunken tubs surrounded by lots of windows.

Big Ideas

The very nature of large homes requires considerable thought about use of space. Having a large home simply for size doesn't necessarily mean gaining more usable space. Room layouts, along with window and door placement, have a lot to do with how well any home functions. Buyers who don't take some of these things into consideration may find themselves wandering around in a lot of space.

Make sure you need all the space. Many buyers know the home they are currently living in is too small for them. They want bigger, but how much bigger? Some people have a hard time understanding the true size and volume of a building.

Large-scale home design typically incorporates expansive, tall, open areas. Great care should be taken to achieve the desired effect but not at the risk of creating an uncomfortable living atmosphere with echoes and poor heating and cooling conditions. Also, some customers desire structural features that pose problems from engineering and construction aspects.

Above all, keep in mind that there is always more than one way to achieve a certain look or feature. The key is to find an economical and practical approach to the design.

Relying on the experience and expertise of professional designers will go a long way toward assuring that you wind up with a large home that is grand yet makes sense.

Most importantly, make sure that any design enables you to get the most home for your money. That should always be your goal, no matter what size home you dream of owning.

Here is a list of design elements that are most popular— often expected— in the creation of a large home:

- **Great Rooms:** Large, expansive living rooms typically open to kitchens and dining rooms. In many cases, great rooms feature tall walls of glass that take advantage of views. Opening the entry foyer to this room gives guests a grand impression upon entering the home.

- **Covered Entry Porches with Built-up Columns**

- **Sky Walls and Sun Spaces:** Such features are popular for large, high-end homes, kitchens, breakfast nooks and spas or poolrooms.

- **Bonus Rooms:** Large-scale homes are expected to offer extra rooms, computer stations with built-in desks, walk-in pantries and his-and-her walk-in closets adjacent to deluxe master bathrooms. Wine cellars are also popular.

- **Grand Staircases:** Available in many styles, configurations and prices, stairs are an important statement for high-end homes.

- **Exposed Timber Structures:** Even homes that are not built with logs feature exposed beams and structural members in great rooms and recreation rooms. For the solid-timber and log-home market, this detail is a natural. The only questions is: how much and where?

Nantucket

Double decks, porches, multiple entries, a daylight basement, and a guest suite, playroom and workout room over the garage are all areas that extend the living spaces of the "Nantucket" from Moose Creek Log Homes. It boasts 6,960 total square feet.

Plan Title: **Nantucket**

Home Size: **6,960 square feet**

Plan Designer: **Moose Creek Log Homes**

For more information, contact
Moose Creek Log Homes, Turner, Maine;
phone: 800-625-6446;
website: www.moosecreekloghomes.com.

The main level is designed as one flowing great room that extends to a sitting area beyond the breakfast nook and a study beside the stairs off the formal entry. This busy layout draws the eye in many directions, but ultimately to the stairway. It climbs to a second-story master suite that features a private deck and a lounging area overlooking the great room.

An additional guest suite, playroom and workout room extend over the garage. The daylight basement adds additional living and recreational space, plus a roomy wine cellar.

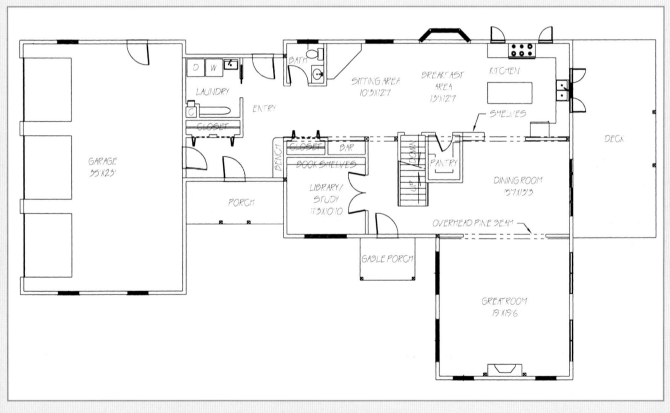

MAIN FLOOR PLAN

Nantucket

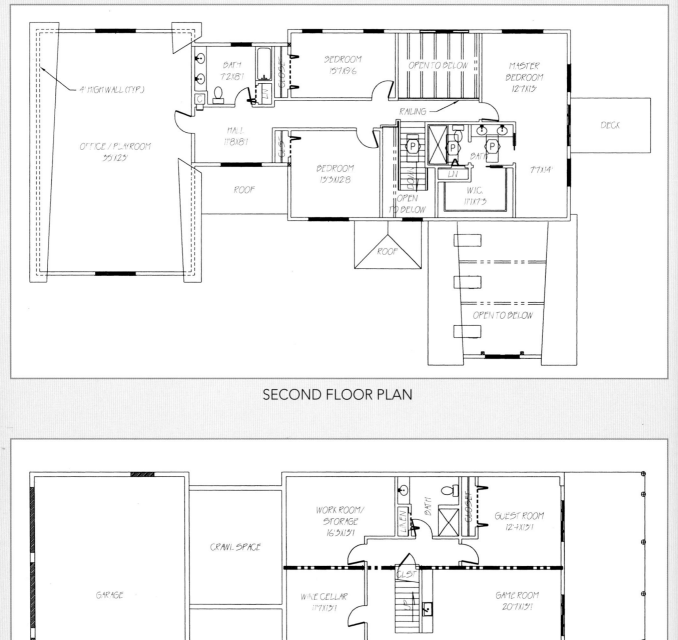

4' HIGH WALL (TYP.)

BATH
7'2X8'1

BEDROOM
15'7X9'6

OPEN TO BELOW

MASTER
BEDROOM
12'7X13'

OFFICE / PLAYROOM
35'X23'

HALL
11'8X8'1

RAILING

DECK

BEDROOM
13'3X12'8

ROOF

BATH
7'7X14'

OPEN
TO BELOW

W.I.C.
11'1X7'3

ROOF

OPEN TO BELOW

SECOND FLOOR PLAN

GARAGE

CRAWL SPACE

WORK ROOM/
STORAGE
16'3X13'1

BATH

GUEST ROOM
12'7X13'1

LINEN

CLST

WINE CELLAR
11'7X13'1

GAME ROOM
20'7X13'1

REC. ROOM
18'8X20'

LOWER LEVEL FLOOR PLAN

The main level of the "Nantucket" is a flowing great room. A lounging area off of the second-story master suite overlooks this room.

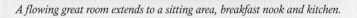

A flowing great room extends to a sitting area, breakfast nook and kitchen.

Mountain Magnificence

There's nothing like a large entryway, foyer and covered porch to greet visitors, welcoming them into a home.

Plan Title: **Mountain Magnificence**

Home Size: **6,986 square feet**

Plan Designer: **Alpine Log Homes**

For more information, contact Alpine Log Homes, Victor, Montana; phone: 406-642-3451; website: www.alpineloghomes.com.

A rambling layout relies on angles to distinguish interior space. The core is the stepped-down great room topped by a vaulted ceiling. Two wings split off it. The first leads to a master suite that is more of a separate apartment, featuring the bedroom, bath and twin walk-in closets, but also a bump-out sitting room. An office in the master wing enjoys privacy.

The other wing contains a three-car garage, but above it is a bunkroom able to accommodate 12 children. Above the kitchen, at the top of the stairs, is a crafts studio with its own deck, which tops the downstairs breakfast nook.

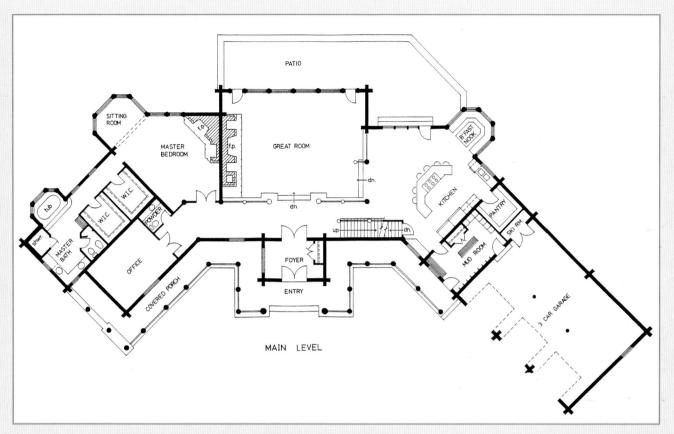

MAIN FLOOR PLAN

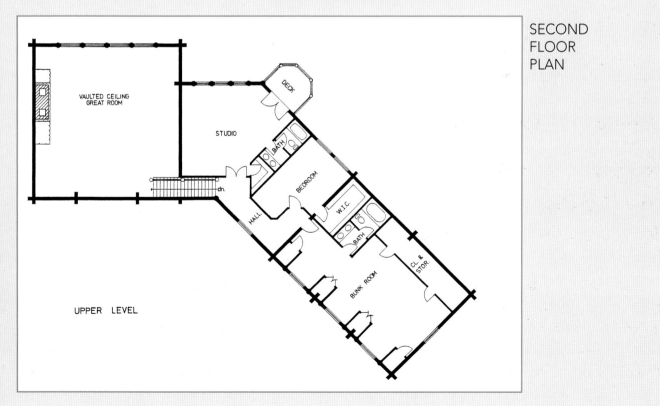

SECOND
FLOOR
PLAN

Mountain Magnificence

The great room and kitchen of the Alpine Log Homes "Mountain Magnificence" open onto the patio.

The core of the Alpine Log Homes "Mountain Magnificence" model is the stepped-down great room topped by a vaulted ceiling.

Rutherford

The striking exterior lines of the Southland Log Homes "Rutherford" mark a compartmentalized layout that offers plenty of living space, plus several handy hideaways.

Plan Title: **Rutherford**

Home Size: **5,638 square feet**

Plan Designer: **Southland Log Homes**

For more information, contact
Southland Log Homes, Irmo, South Carolina;
phone: 800-828-1492;
website: www.southlandloghomes.com.

Striking exterior lines mark a compartmentalized layout that offers plenty of living space, plus several handy hideaways. The highlight is the kitchen, which enjoys a breakfast nook, oversized pantry, sunroom and grilling deck. Off the nook is a study with a half bath.

The foyer leads through to the great room, but before that is the dining room and a small living room. Serving the master bedroom is a 248-square-foot master bath. The second story boasts a playroom above the three-car garage, three bedrooms, three baths and a balcony overlooking the foyer and great room.

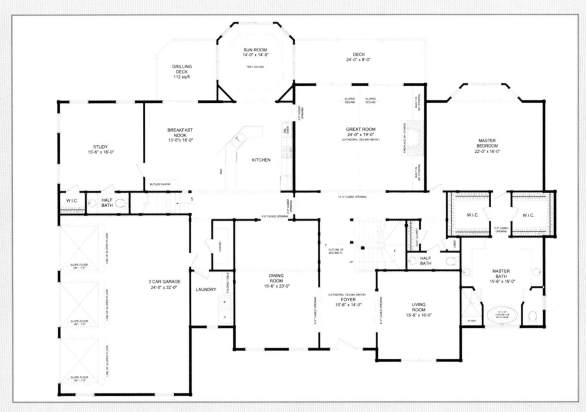

FIRST FLOOR PLAN

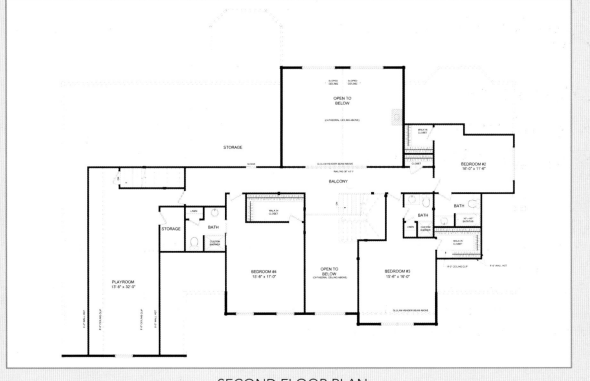

SECOND FLOOR PLAN

Plans With More Than 4,000 Square Feet · **193**

DeSoto

The DeSoto's dormers and windows definitely create a dynamic exterior.

Plan Title: **DeSoto**

Home Size: **5,707 square feet**

Plan Designer: **Kuhns Bros. Log Homes**

For more information, contact
Kuhns Bros. Log Homes, Lewisburg, Pennsylvania;
phone: 800-326-9614;
website: www.kuhnsbros.com.

This spacious layout features plenty of windows and dormers to create a dynamic exterior. Inside, the foyer opens to a massive staircase leading to a panoramic loft and, beyond the stairs, a great room filled with windows for light and views.

Balancing the roomy master suite wing are the combined kitchen and dining area and a tucked-away office. A generous mudroom/laundry room transitions to the three-bay garage. Upstairs, mirror-image bedrooms occupy the wings flanking the loft, which showcases a series of timber trusses.

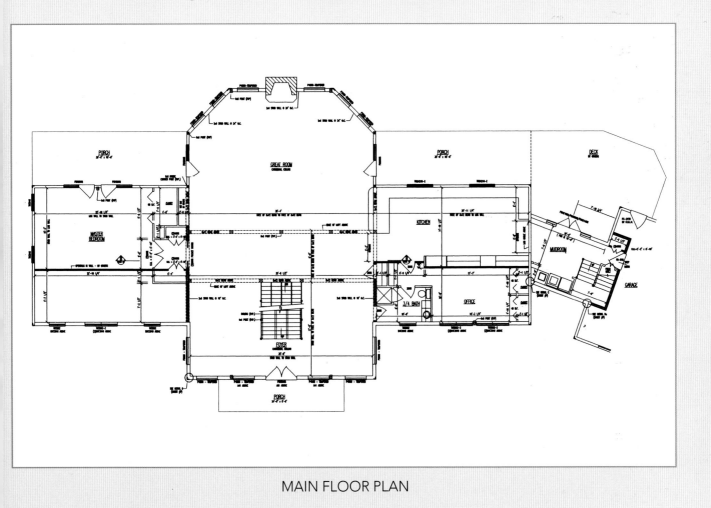

MAIN FLOOR PLAN

DeSoto

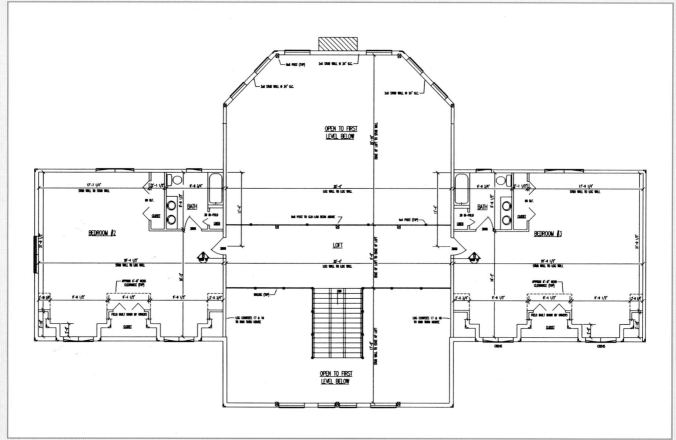

SECOND FLOOR PLAN

The master bedroom is on the first floor of the DeSoto and two more, mirror-image bedrooms occupy the wings flanking the loft.

A panoramic loft overlooks the dining room, part of an open concept with high ceilings.

The foyer opens to a massive staircase leading to the loft.

Plenty of windows allow outdoor light to penetrate the spacious dining and living room of the Kuhns Bros. Log Homes "DeSoto."

The roomy office of the Kuhns Bros. Log Homes "DeSoto" is tucked away off the kitchen.

Schmidt

Dramatic ridgelines and circle-top windows define the Kuhns Bros. Log Homes "Schmidt."

Plan Title: **Schmidt**

Home Size: **4,294 square feet**

Plan Designer: **Kuhns Bros. Log Homes**

For more information, contact Kuhns Bros. Log Homes, Lewisburg, Pennsylvania; phone: 800-326-9614; website: www.kuhnsbros.com.

Circle-top windows and dramatic ridgelines stand out in this semi-open plan. It includes the master suite, which, in addition to a room-sized bath and walk-in closets, has a private office with tall, round-top windows and a sunroom.

The corner kitchen and adjacent dining area, both topped with a timber-beam ceiling, access a screened porch. Upstairs, two bedrooms share a spacious bath. The loft opens to a generous storage area that could also serve as a sewing or hobby room.

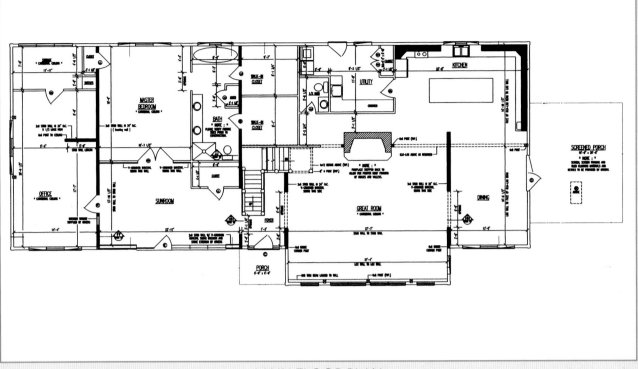

MAIN FLOOR PLAN

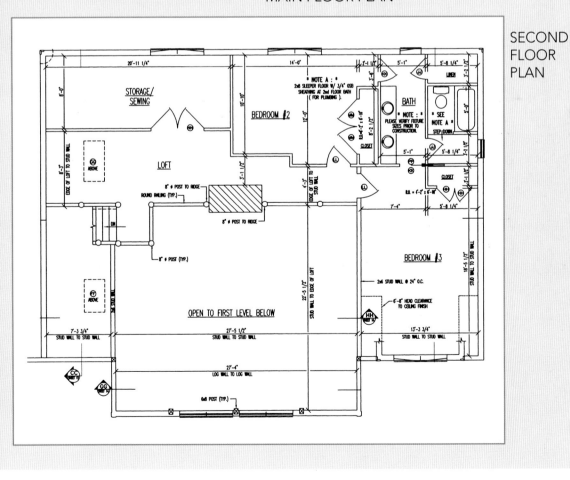

SECOND
FLOOR
PLAN

Schmidt

Windows, a two-story ceiling and exposed beams benefit the five-sided great room of the "Schmidt."

The private office shows off tall, round-top windows.

The kitchen and adjacent dining room of the "Schmidt" are topped with timber-beam ceilings and have access to a screened porch.

The two upstairs bedrooms of the "Schmidt" share a spacious bath.

Plans With More Than 4,000 Square Feet ·

Hickory Ridge

A loft space overlooks the living room of "Hickory Ridge."

Plan Title: **Hickory Ridge**

Home Size: **4,503 square feet**

Plan Designer: **Hearthstone**

For more information, contact
Hearthstone, Dandridge, Tennessee;
phone: 800-247-4442;
website: www.hearthstonehomes.com.

A roomy foyer in this compartmentalized plan leads to a cozy living room, which opens to the kitchen, stairs and a second entry. A separate wing behind the island kitchen is set aside for formal dining.

The master suite accesses the rear porch and an office or den. Three bedrooms and two baths on the second level have a large laundry room and a loft space overlooking the living room. The stairs continue to a third-level loft.

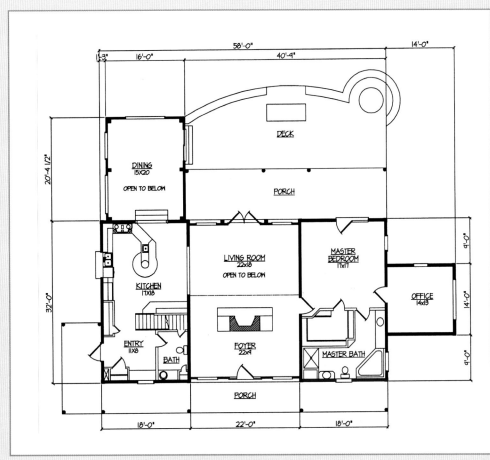

MAIN FLOOR PLAN

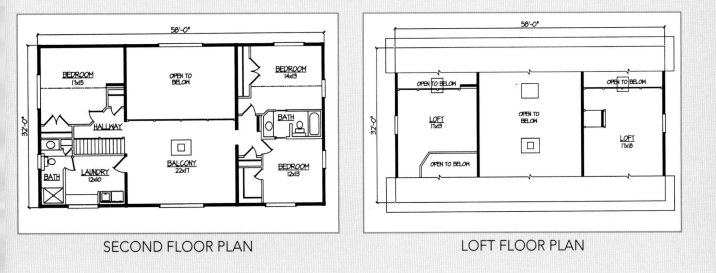

SECOND FLOOR PLAN

LOFT FLOOR PLAN

Hickory Ridge

A roomy foyer in the compartmentalized "Hickory Ridge" leads to the living room.

The master bedroom accesses the rear porch and an office or den.

An inviting tub beckons in the master bath.

Three bedrooms upstairs provide plenty of living and sleeping space for large families.

A porch, deck and multiple, flowing and inviting rooflines, including shed dormers, give the Hearthstone Maine Cabin a homey feel.

Plan Title: **Maine Cabin**

Home Size: **4,240 square feet**

Plan Designer: **Hearthstone**

For more information, contact
Hearthstone, Dandridge, Tennessee;
phone: 800-247-4442;
website: www.hearthstonehomes.com.

Noteworthy about this plan is the roomy living area, which is positioned between the kitchen and a dining room beside the main entry. The main focal point is the fireplace with two fireboxes, one serving the kitchen. The great room steps down into a generous sunroom, which is also accessible from the side deck.

Upstairs, a spacious office area with shed dormer accesses its own deck. This level also features a bedroom and bathroom with stall shower. A walkout basement includes a media room, home office, an exercise room, half bath and abundant storage space.

Maine Cabin

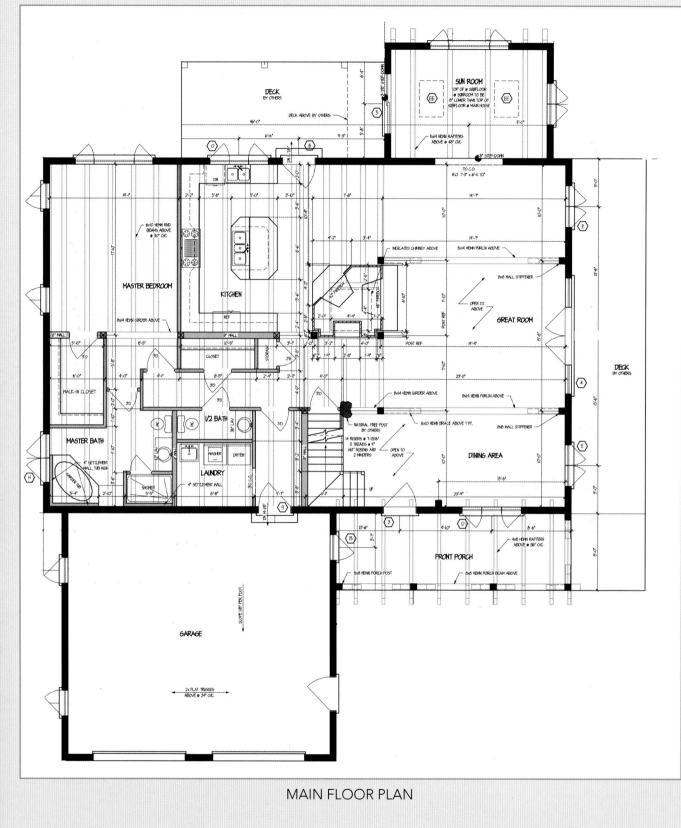

MAIN FLOOR PLAN

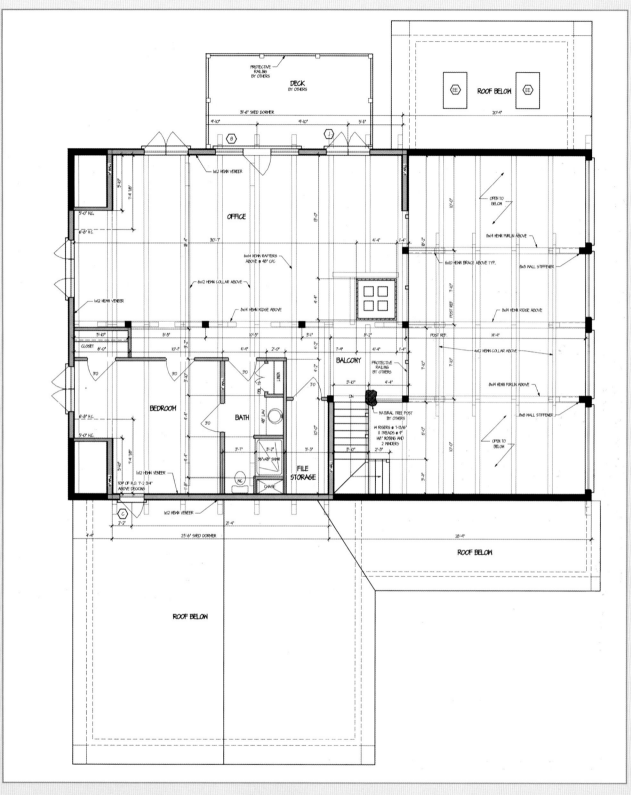

SECOND FLOOR PLAN

Maine Cabin

One side of the Hearthstone "Main Cabin" fireplace serves the kitchen.

Upstairs, a spacious office area with shed dormer accesses its own deck.

One noteworthy aspect of the Hearthstone "Maine Cabin" is the roomy living area.

The upstairs features a bedroom and a bathroom with a stall shower.

The great room is positioned between the kitchen and a dining room beside the main entry.

The Iron Mountain

At 4,318 square feet, there's room in the layout and design of "The Iron Mountain" from Hearthstone for a large covered patio in front, complete with a two-sided fireplace, one side facing out to the patio, and the other facing inside to the great room.

Plan Title: **The Iron Mountain**

Home Size: **4,318 square feet**

Plan Designer: **Hearthstone**

For more information, contact
Hearthstone, Dandridge, Tennessee;
phone: 800-247-4442;
website: www.hearthstonehomes.com.

The open floor plan has easy access to the kitchen, dining and living areas. The main-level master suite accesses a patio. The two-sided fireplace serves the great room and a covered patio, and a third patio is located off the kitchen. A transition area between the kitchen and garage includes a deep pantry, half bath, laundry room and mudroom.

Upstairs comprises a loft, a guest suite, a second large bedroom, an additional bathroom and a huge bonus room above the garage.

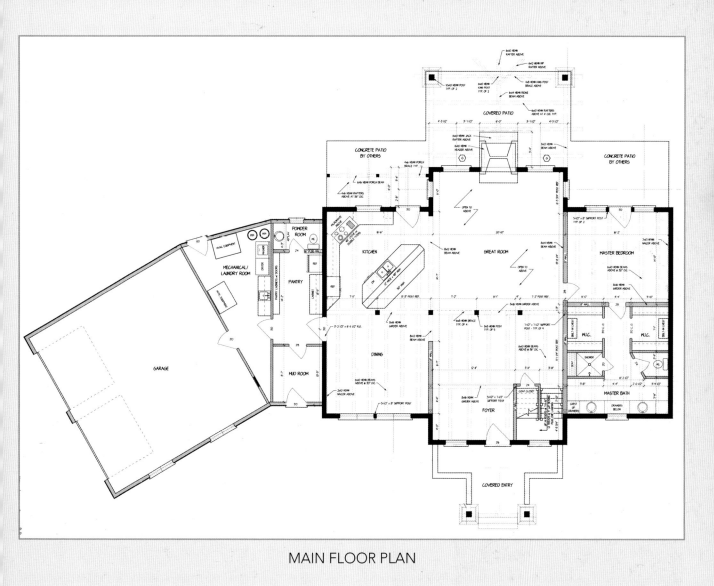

MAIN FLOOR PLAN

The Iron Mountain

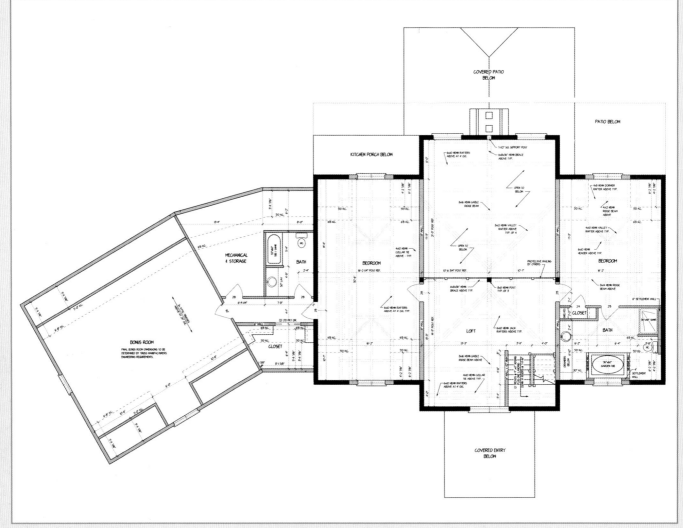

SECOND FLOOR PLAN

The main-level master suite, including its own bathroom, accesses a patio.

The open floor plan of "The Iron Mountain" includes easy access to the kitchen, dining and living areas.

The Iron Mountain

Upstairs comprises a loft, a guest suite, a second large bedroom, an additional bathroom and a huge bonus room above the garage.

The Skaneateles

The semi-compartmentalized layout of the Beaver Mountain Log & Cedar Homes "The Skaneateles" takes advantage of the space above the garage for a generous master suite, freeing the downstairs for an expansive great room, formal entry, a screened porch off the dining room, and adjacent family room and office.

Plan Title: **The Skaneateles**

Home Size: **4,112 square feet**

Plan Designer: **Beaver Mountain Log & Cedar Homes**

For more information, contact
Beaver Mountain Log & Cedar Homes,
Hancock, New York;
phone: 800-233-2770;
website: www.beavermtn.com.

This semi-compartmentalized layout takes advantage of the space above the garage for a generous master suite, freeing the downstairs for an expansive great room, formal entry, a screened porch off the dining room, and adjacent family room and office.

Dormers enlarge the upstairs, which, besides the master suite, features two bedrooms with private baths and a roomy loft, open to the great room at one end and leading to a balcony porch at the other.

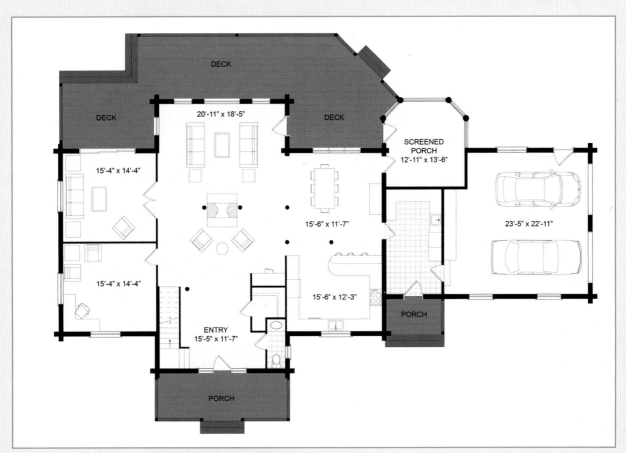

DECK

DECK

20'-11" x 18'-5"

DECK

SCREENED
PORCH
12'-11" x 13'-6"

15'-4" x 14'-4"

23'-5" x 22'-11"

15'-6" x 11'-7"

15'-4" x 14'-4"

15'-6" x 12'-3"

PORCH

ENTRY
15'-5" x 11'-7"

PORCH

MAIN FLOOR PLAN

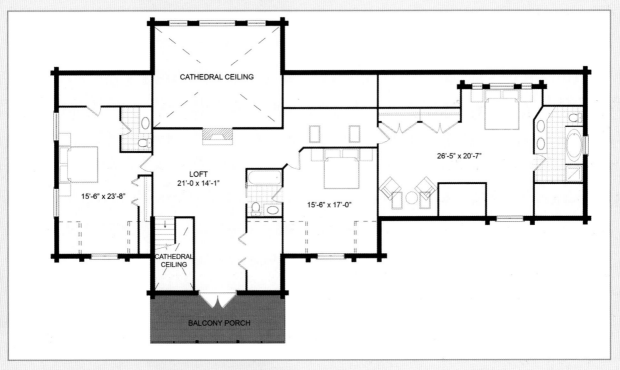

CATHEDRAL CEILING

26'-5" x 20'-7"

LOFT
21'-0 x 14'-1"

15'-6" x 23'-8"

15'-6" x 17'-0"

CATHEDRAL
CEILING

BALCONY PORCH

SECOND FLOOR PLAN

Plans With More Than 4,000 Square Feet · **217**

The McKinley

The boomerang configuration of "The McKinley" from Tennessee Log Homes spreads the model out so more rooms enjoy a view.

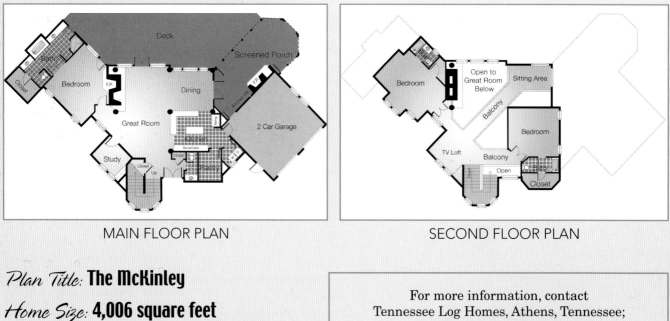

MAIN FLOOR PLAN   SECOND FLOOR PLAN

Plan Title: **The McKinley**

Home Size: **4,006 square feet**

Plan Designer: **Tennessee Log Homes**

For more information, contact
Tennessee Log Homes, Athens, Tennessee;
phone: 800-251-9218;
website: www.tnloghomes.com.

The boomerang configuration of this layout spreads the home out so more rooms enjoy a view. The entryway stands out with its octagonal turret. In addition to the main-level master suite, which accesses the patio from either the bedroom or the bath, the home has two junior master suites upstairs.

The ample square footage permits a private study off the great room and a pantry serving the kitchen. The garage and dining room enjoy access to the screened porch. The upstairs bedrooms share a loft, which features a catwalk that leads to a private space overlooking the patio.

The expansive plan of "The Warner" from Original Old Timer Log Homes & Supply includes four bedrooms, and an open kitchen and living area.

Plan Title: **The Warner**

Home Size: **5,228 square feet**

Plan Designer:

Original Old Timer Log Homes & Supply

For more information, contact
Original Old Timer Log Homes & Supply,
Mount Juliet, Tennessee; phone: 800-467-3006;
website: www.oldtimerloghomes.com.

This roomy plan includes four bedrooms, an open kitchen and living area and built-in storage space. In the great room, high ceilings enhance winding stairs. The master suite with fireplace has spiral stairs ascending to a private loft that is a retreat in and of itself.

Two large main-level bedrooms share a bath behind the kitchen/dining room. A large utility room separates the house and garage. Dormers add headroom to the upper level, which features a junior master suite.

The Warner features a large, second-floor bedroom.

The Warner

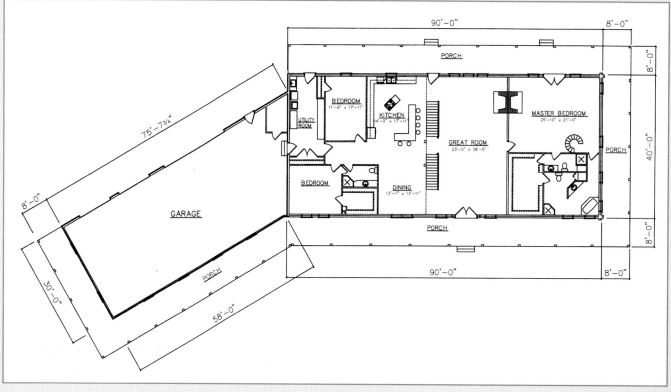

MAIN FLOOR PLAN

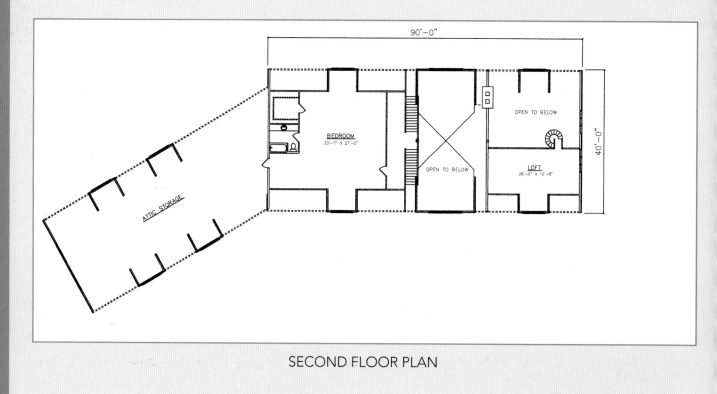

SECOND FLOOR PLAN

The master suite with fireplace has spiral stairs that ascend to a private loft—a retreat in and of itself.

Dormers add headroom to the upper level, which features a junior master suite.

The open kitchen and dining room help "The Warner" achieve a spacious interior.

Mountain View

The walkout lower level of the "Mountain View" offers plenty of living space in addition to the main and upper floors.

Plan Title: **Mountain View**

Home Size: **4,108 square feet**

Plan Designer: **Strongwood Log Home Company**

For more, contact
Strongwood Log Home Company,
Waupaca, Wisconsin; phone: 866-258-4818;
website: www.strongwoodloghome.com.

The spacious great room, highlighted by an end wall of windows, dominates the layout, which is noteworthy for the large circular staircase that winds from the lower level to the loft in an octagonal turret. The loft offers more than 500 square feet of bonus space.

The luxurious master suite enjoys complete privacy, while guest rooms are located above the garage, which is linked to the home by a patio. The walkout lower level offers plenty of living space in addition to the main and upper floors.

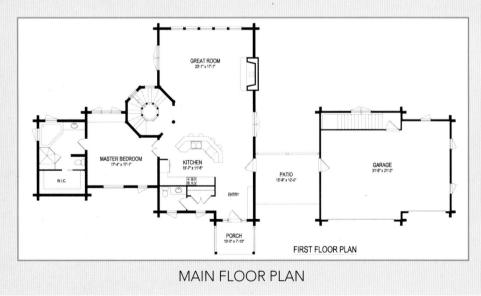

MAIN FLOOR PLAN

Windows, bump-outs, a large covered entry and multiple rooflines characterize "The Big Creek" from Neville Log Homes.

Plan Title: **The Big Creek**

Home Size: **7,077 square feet**

Plan Designer: **Neville Log Homes**

For more, contact
Neville Log Homes, Victor, Montana;
phone: 800-635-7911; website: www.nevilog.com.

The ship-shaped great room and dining area form the centerpiece of the home, topped by two scissors trusses and adjoining a spacious kitchen and roomy foyer. A spiral staircase punctuates the foyer. Angled off the other side is the palatial, 800-square-foot master suite, which has a screened porch and hot tub, deck, another porch and an office.

The modest loft features a powder room and lanai, whereas the sprawling lower level comprises four bedrooms, three bathrooms, a kitchenette, exercise room and a large family room.

The Big Creek

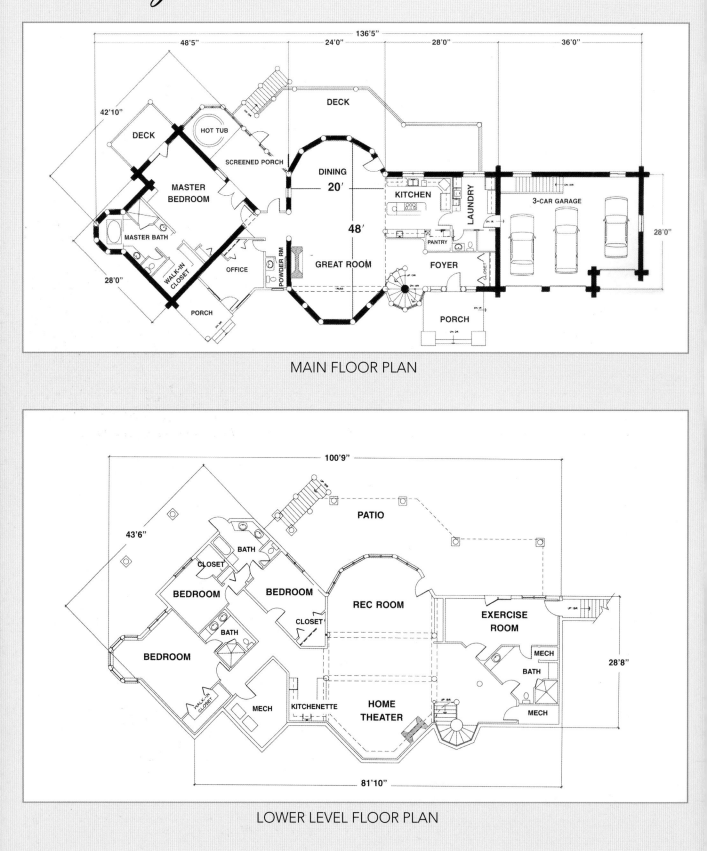

MAIN FLOOR PLAN

LOWER LEVEL FLOOR PLAN

The ship-shaped great room and dining area of "The Big Creek" form the centerpiece of the home, topped by two scissors trusses.

The palatial, 800-square-foot master suite includes a master bath, screened porch/hot-tub room, deck, office and another porch.

The Bitterroot

Plan Title: **The Bitterroot**

Home Size: **4,300 square feet**

Plan Designer: **Neville Log Homes**

For more, contact
Neville Log Homes, Victor, Montana;
phone: 800-635-7911;
website: www.nevilog.com.

Windows surround the great room, which is the cornerstone of this semi-open plan. Generous space is also provided on the lower level for a formal entry, three bedrooms and a den.

Outside, extensive decks and porches extend the home's living space. A special touch is an outside spiral staircase that leads to the second-floor master suite, which has a private library, abundant storage space and a loft sitting area. A porte-cochere offers protection for arriving vehicles.

Windows surround the great room of "The Bitterroot" from Neville Log Homes, and extensive decks and porches extend the home's living space.

The Bitterroot

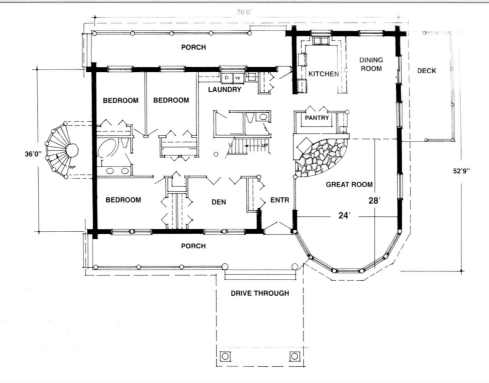

MAIN FLOOR PLAN

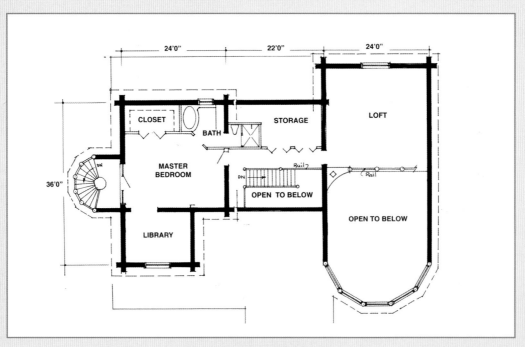

SECOND FLOOR PLAN

Depending on which of the three bedrooms or master suite one is staying, they might literally end up in a room with a view.

The open-concept kitchen is a cozy spot for drinking morning coffee or enjoying a midday lunch at the counter.

The Telluride

Contemporary styling with a rustic, Western feel is a good description of "The Telluride" from Neville Log Homes.

Plan Title: **The Telluride**

Home Size: **5,209 square feet**

Plan Designer: **Neville Log Homes**

For more, contact
Neville Log Homes, Victor, Montana;
phone: 800-635-7911;
website: www.nevilog.com.

This spacious, three-level home combines contemporary styling with a rustic, Western feel. The main floor contains a foyer, living room, kitchen/dining area and laundry room. The laundry room leads to an angled wing containing three bedrooms and baths.

The space above the angled wing houses the entire master suite, with its own deck. A walkway leads to a balcony overlooking the great room and an honest-to-goodness bunkroom. The lower level boasts a huge family room, a media room, a full bath, wet bar and an additional fireplace.

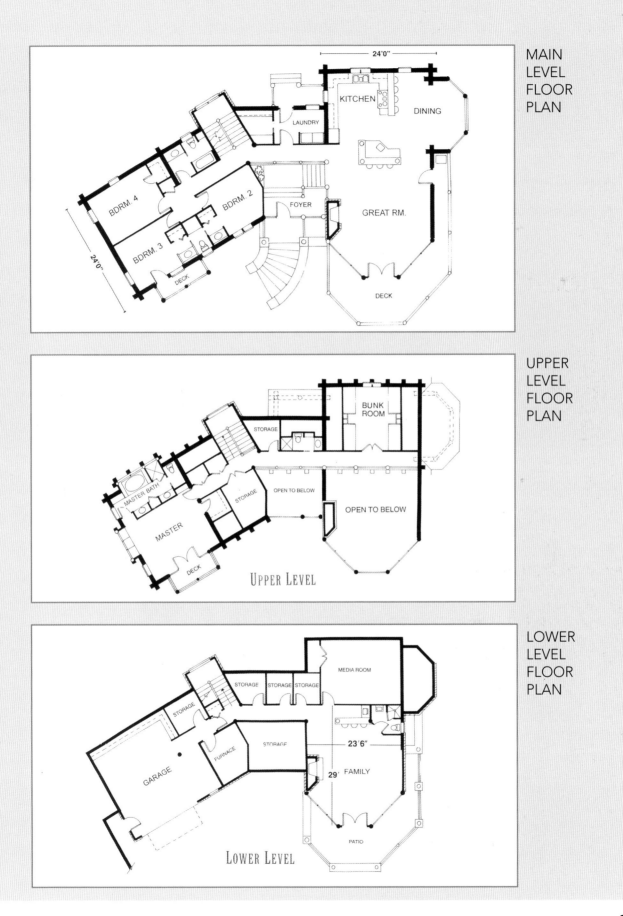

MAIN
LEVEL
FLOOR
PLAN

UPPER
LEVEL
FLOOR
PLAN

LOWER
LEVEL
FLOOR
PLAN

Alpine Meadow II

Twin dormers flanking a wall of windows in the great room lend exterior drama to the Wisconsin Log Homes "Alpine Meadow II."

Plan Title: Alpine Meadow II

Home Size: 4,334 square feet

Plan Designer: Wisconsin Log Homes

For more, contact
Wisconsin Log Homes, Green Bay, Wisconsin;
phone: 800-844-7970;
website: www.wisconsinloghomes.com.

Twin dormers flanking a wall of windows in the great room lend exterior drama to this design. Inside, the central great room opens to the kitchen and dining room and adjoins the master suite. The master bedroom, living room and dining room enjoy access to the wraparound deck.

Upstairs, an open loft with built-in wet bar splits two bedrooms and baths, while guests enjoy privacy tucked behind a large bonus room.

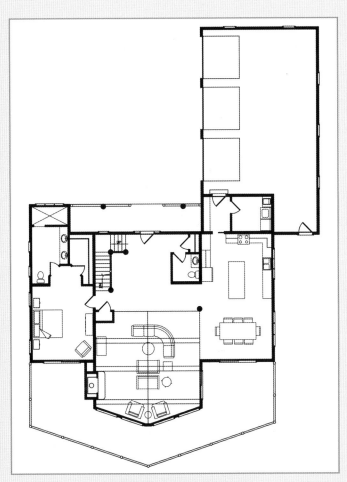

MAIN FLOOR PLAN

SECOND FLOOR PLAN

The central great room opens to the kitchen and dining room.

The well-windowed great room of the "Alpine Meadow II" adjoins the master suite.

Upstairs, an open loft splits two bedrooms and baths.

The Summit

Adding interest to the profile of "The Summit" are a varied roofline and six balconies.

Plan Title: The Summit

Home Size: 4,711 square feet

Plan Designer: Yellowstone Log Homes

For more, contact
Yellowstone Log Homes, Rigby, Idaho;
phone: 208-745-8108;
website: www.yellowstoneloghomes.com.

A varied roofline and six balconies add interest to the home's profile, while inside a compartmentalized layout allows for a variety of rooms. The central great room balances windows and fireplace as focal points and leads to a kitchen/dining area that features a glass-surrounded breakfast nook. To the left of the entry are a generous family room and separate office.

The mudroom leads to a breezeway that accesses a two-car garage, adding another 720 square feet. Five bedrooms are upstairs, including a luxurious master suite.

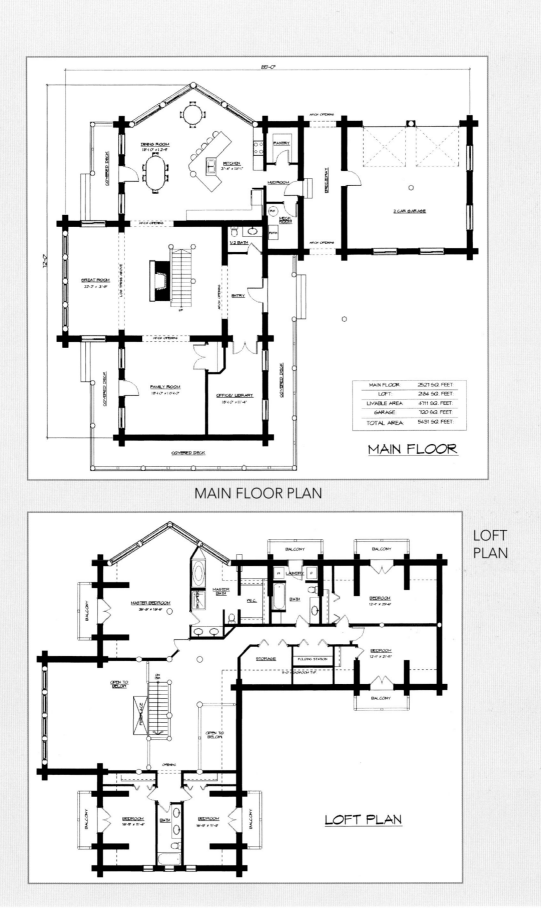

MAIN FLOOR PLAN

MAIN FLOOR:	2521 SQ. FEET.
LOFT:	2184 SQ. FEET.
LIVABLE AREA:	4711 SQ. FEET.
GARAGE:	720 SQ. FEET.
TOTAL AREA:	5431 SQ. FEET.

MAIN FLOOR

LOFT PLAN

LOFT PLAN

Extreme Makeover

The first log home featured on the network television show "Extreme Makeover: Home Edition," the thoughtfully organized plan features three levels with a gazebo and a large wraparound deck.

Plan Title: Extreme Makeover
Home Size: 4,398 square feet
Plan Designer: Katahdin Cedar Log Homes

For more, contact
Katahdin Cedar Log Homes,
Oakfield, Maine; phone: 800-845-4533;
website: www.katahdincedarloghomes.com.

This thoughtfully organized plan was the first log home featured on the network television show "Extreme Makeover: Home Edition." It features three levels, with a gazebo and a large wraparound deck offering spectacular views.

Other distinctive features include a main-floor family room with cathedral ceilings and a second-floor loft with a generous master suite. The family room is supplemented by a smaller living room next to the dining area. The optional lower level has two large spaces surrounding a mudroom and laundry room.

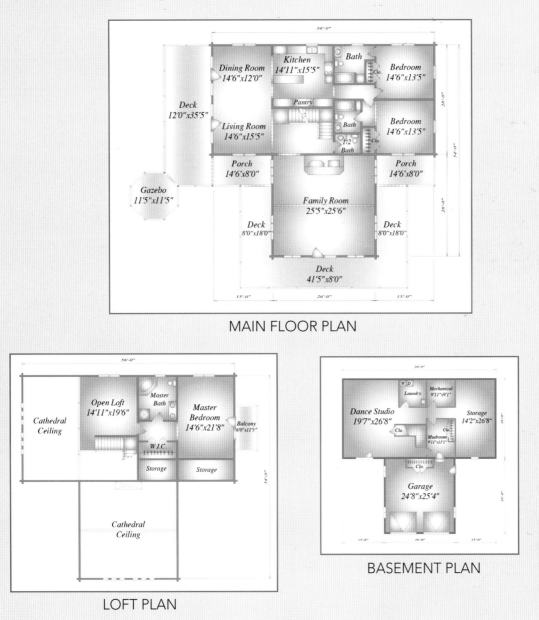

MAIN FLOOR PLAN

LOFT PLAN

BASEMENT PLAN

Moose Lodge

Such features as a truss-covered foyer, a log purlin roof system and a towering cathedral ceiling help set off the Katahdin Cedar Log Homes "Moose Lodge."

Plan Title: **Moose Lodge**

Home Size: **5,178 square feet**

Plan Designer: **Katahdin Cedar Log Homes**

For more, contact
Katahdin Cedar Log Homes,
Oakfield, Maine; phone: 800-845-4533;
website: www.katahdincedarloghomes.com.

Angled wings distinguish this accommodating layout. The step-down living room off the generous, truss-covered foyer features a log purlin roof system with a towering cathedral ceiling.

The kitchen, dining area and a small bedroom separate the living room from an enclosed porch/sunroom and, beyond, the attached garage. The garage transitions to the house through a ski room and breezeway. An opposite wing is dedicated to the master suite, and upstairs, a roomy loft unites twin bedrooms, each with its own bath.

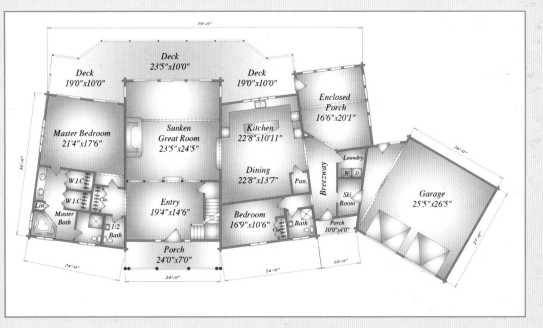

MAIN FLOOR PLAN

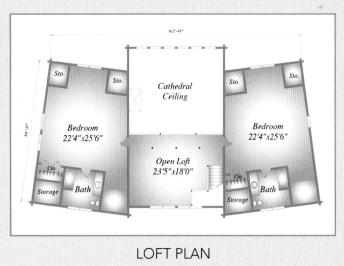

LOFT PLAN

Moose Lodge

The step-down living room is entered through the generous, truss-covered foyer.

A large arched doorway acts as an entrance to the kitchen with fully exposed log beams and a view to the massive fireplace in the living room.

A towering cathedral ceiling, as well as a wall of windows and generous fireplace, allows the living room to literally live large.

West

Sprawling but appealing is a good way to describe the StoneMill Log Homes "West," a winged model with a centralized, spacious great room.

Plan Title: **West**

Home Size: **6,051 square feet**

Plan Designer: **StoneMill Log Homes**

For more, contact StoneMill Log Homes, Knoxville, Tennessee; phone: 800-438-8274; website: www. stonemill.com.

The core of this plan is the spacious great room, which is surrounded by a sequence of rooms. Foremost is the angled master suite wing, which connects to an exercise room and a TV room/office. The bedroom portion enjoys a cathedral ceiling and stairs that climb to a loft.

Balancing this wing is the garage, which attaches through a mudroom off the kitchen. On the upper level, the space above the garage features a fully equipped guest apartment with kitchenette and private balcony. Two more bedrooms fill out the space, much of which is open to the great room.

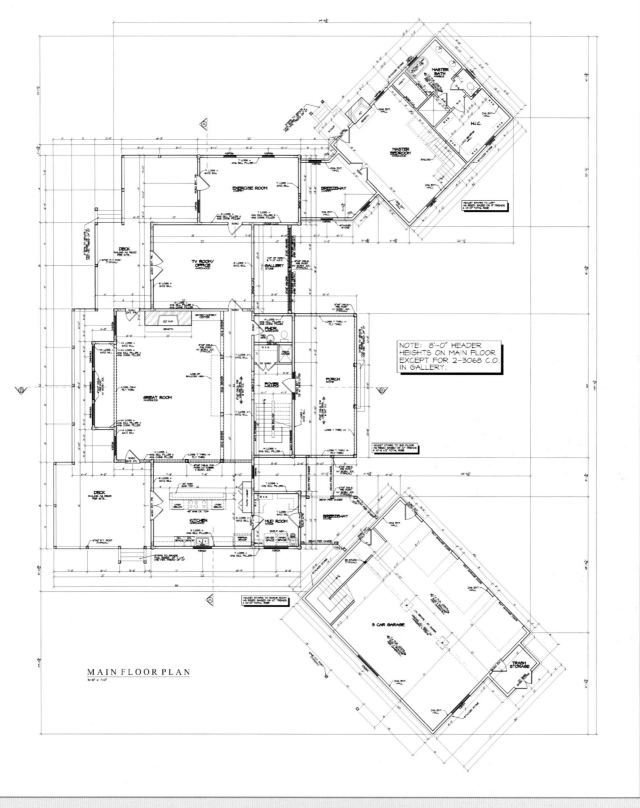

MAIN FLOOR PLAN

NOTE: 8'-0" HEADER
HEIGHTS ON MAIN FLOOR
EXCEPT FOR 2-3068 C.O.
IN GALLERY.

MAIN FLOOR PLAN

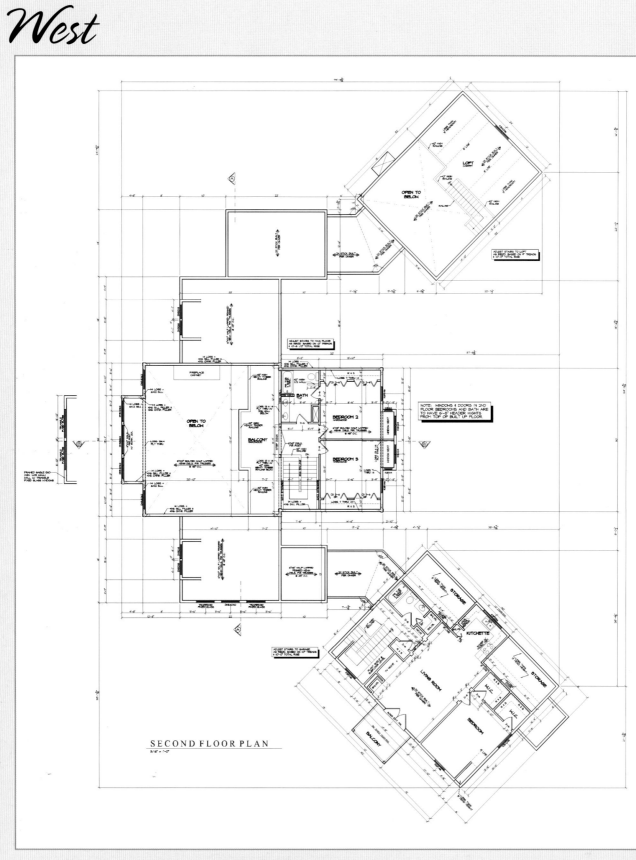

SECOND FLOOR PLAN

SECOND FLOOR PLAN

The spacious great room is the core of the plan.

A vaulted ceiling, dining counter, large windows and access to a deck are a few amenities of the "West" kitchen.

An angled master suite includes a bedroom with a cathedral ceiling and stairs that climb to a loft.

A TV room / office is part of the master suite.

Plans With More Than 4,000 Square Feet ·

The Trailside

"The Trailside" from PrecisionCraft Log Homes and Mountain Architects is a sprawling model with covered porches, multiple rooflines, dormers and much more.

Plan Title: **The Trailside**

Home Size: **4,004 square feet**

Plan Designer: **PrecisionCraft Log Homes and Mountain Architects**

For more, contact
PrecisionCraft Log & Timber Homes and Mountain Architects,
Meridian, Idaho; phone: 800-729-1320; website: www.precisioncraft.com.

The sprawling plan adds comfort to the master suite by providing twin baths and walk-in closets, as well as a fireplace and access to its own porch. The great room lies in the back of the home through an entry hall that encloses a TV room.

Upstairs, two bedrooms have their own baths and walk-in closets, leaving plenty of open space above the living room. A large dormer brightens the front bedroom. A garage attaches to the home through a mudroom and laundry, which are accessible through the kitchen or TV room.

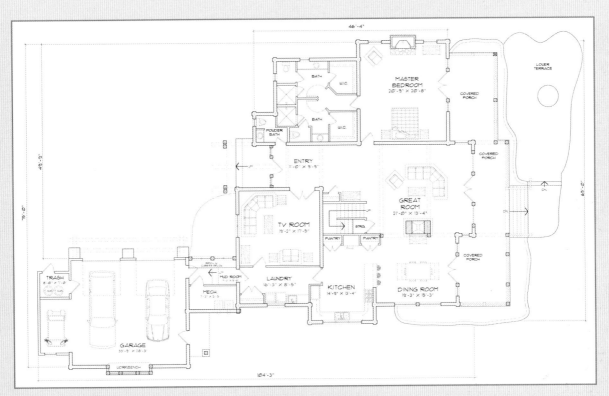

MAIN FLOOR PLAN

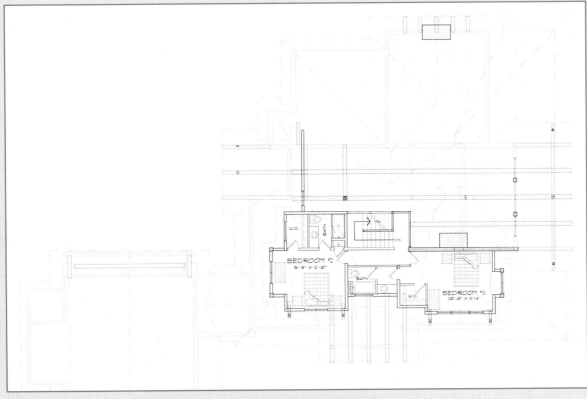

SECOND FLOOR PLAN

Payton

Front and rear dormers, and a wall of windows staring out from the great room are just a couple features of the Real Log Homes "Payton."

Plan Title: **Payton**

Home Size: **5,112 square feet**

Plan Designer: **Real Log Homes**

For more, contact
Real Log Homes, Hartland, Vermont;
phone: 800-732-5564;
website: www.realloghomes.com.

This centralized plan revolves around the great room, which leads to the dining room and kitchen in one wing and a spacious master suite in the other. The kitchen accesses, through the laundry room, a screened porch that connects to an optional, 900-square-foot garage.

The great room, boasting a wall of windows, cathedral ceiling and exposed log rafters, uses an oversized fireplace and stairs to separate it from a foyer that is entered through a dramatic front porch.

Above the foyer is a loft, flanked by two bedrooms and baths, which, in turn, are over the master suite. A large office and a sewing room top the dining room and kitchen. Front and rear dormers add headroom.

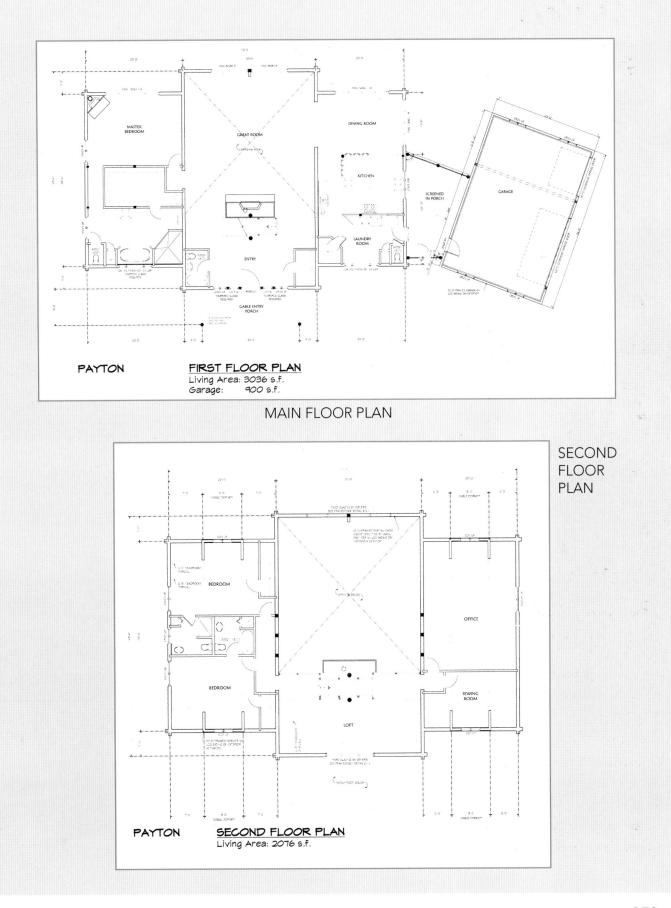

PAYTON   **FIRST FLOOR PLAN**
Living Area: 3036 s.f.
Garage: 900 s.f.

MAIN FLOOR PLAN

SECOND
FLOOR
PLAN

PAYTON   SECOND FLOOR PLAN
Living Area: 2076 s.f.

Payton

The dining room and kitchen of the "Payton" are part of an open concept.

A spacious master suite, including a bath, takes up one wing of the "Payton," and is offset by another wing, which includes the dining room and kitchen.

The great room, boasting a wall of windows, cathedral ceiling and exposed log rafters, uses an oversized fireplace and stairs to separate it from a foyer.

A large office and a sewing room top the dining room and kitchen.

Log Home Manufacturers

Following is a list of manufacturers with log homes featured within the covers of "100 Best Log Home Floor Plans"

Alpine Log Homes; phone: 406-642-3451; website: www.alpineloghomes.com.

Appalachian Log Structures; phone: 800-458-9990; website:www.applog.com.

Beaver Mountain Log & Cedar Homes; phone: 800-233-2770; website: www.beavermtn.com.

Cedarcraft Log Homes; phone: 800-982-2902; website: www.cedarcraftloghomes.com.

Coventry Log Homes; phone: 800-308-7505; website: www.coventryloghomes.com.

Gastineau Log Homes; phone: 800-654-9253; website:www.oakloghome.com.

Golden Eagle Log Homes; phone: 800-270-5025; website: www.goldeneagleloghomes.com.

Hearthstone; phone: 800-247-4442; website:www.hearthstonehomes.com.

Katahdin Cedar Log Homes; phone: 800-845-4533; website: www.katahdincedarloghomes.com.

Kuhns Bros. Log Homes; phone: 800-326-9614; website: www.kuhnsbros.com.

Lodge Logs; phone: 800-533-2450; website:www.lodgelogs.com.

Log Homes of America; phone: 828-963-7777; website: www.loghomesofamerica.com.

Moose Creek Log Homes; phone: 800-625-6446; website: www.moosecreekloghomes.com.

Neville Log Homes; phone: 800-635-7911; website: www.nevilog.com.

Northeastern Log Homes; phone: 800-624-2797; website: www.northeasternlog.com.

Original Old Timer Log Homes & Supply; phone: 800-467-3006; website: www.oldtimerloghomes.com.

PrecisionCraft Log & Timber Homes and Mountain Architects; phone: 800-729-1320; website: www.precisioncraft.com.

Real Log Homes; phone: 800-732-5564; website: www.realloghomes.com.

Southland Log Homes; phone: 800-828-1492; website: www.southlandloghomes.com.

StoneMill Log Homes; phone: 800-438-8274; website: www.stonemill.com.

Strongwood Log Home Co.; phone: 866-258-4818; website: www.strongwoodloghome.com.

Tennessee Log Homes; phone: 800-251-9218; website: www.tnloghomes.com.

Wisconsin Log Homes; phone: 800-844-7970; website: www.wisconsinloghomes.com.

Yellowstone Log Homes; phone: 208-745-8108; website: www.yellowstoneloghomes.com.

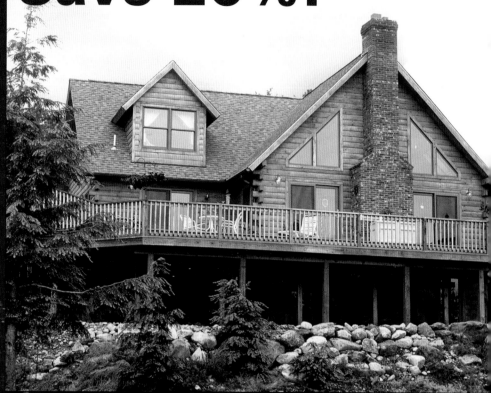